Improving the Army's Management of Reparable Spare Parts

John R. Folkeson, Marygail K. Brauner

Prepared for the United States Army

Approved for public release; distribution unlimited

RAND ARROYO CENTER

The research described in this report was sponsored by the United States Army under Contract No. DASW01-01-C-0003.

ISBN: 0-8330-3743-9

The RAND Corporation is a nonprofit research organization providing objective analysis and effective solutions that address the challenges facing the public and private sectors around the world. RAND's publications do not necessarily reflect the opinions of its research clients and sponsors.

RAND® is a registered trademark.

© Copyright 2005 RAND Corporation

All rights reserved. No part of this book may be reproduced in any form by any electronic or mechanical means (including photocopying, recording, or information storage and retrieval) without permission in writing from RAND.

Published 2005 by the RAND Corporation
1776 Main Street, P.O. Box 2138, Santa Monica, CA 90407-2138
1200 South Hayes Street, Arlington, VA 22202-5050
201 North Craig Street, Suite 202, Pittsburgh, PA 15213-1516
RAND URL: http://www.rand.org/
To order RAND documents or to obtain additional information, contact
Distribution Services: Telephone: (310) 451-7002;
Fax: (310) 451-6915; Email: order@rand.org

Preface

The Army's Velocity Management (VM) initiative was implemented in 1995 to improve the responsiveness, reliability, and efficiency of the Army's logistics system.[1] By applying a simple, yet powerful, process-improvement methodology, the Army dramatically streamlined its field-level supply process and its overall distribution process, cutting median order-fulfillment times for repair parts by nearly two-thirds worldwide and by over 75 percent at several major installations.

This report addresses initial efforts to expand the VM initiative by applying an integrative approach to improving the Army's national-level inventory management and depot-level component-repair processes. The objective of the Army's reparable-management process is to repair sufficient assets to replenish serviceable inventories to meet the needs of requirements determined to support equipment readiness. This report addresses both reparable-inventory planning and the national component-repair activities as an integrated process.

This study should be of interest to those involved with maintenance, supply, resource management, and information systems. The reparable-management process activities discussed have significant interactions across traditional functional management areas (i.e., wholesale-item management, depot maintenance, and financial management). The research was conducted over an extended period and relies upon snapshots of system performance data to describe the process.

This project was jointly sponsored by the Deputy Chief of Staff for Logistics (G4), Headquarters Department of the Army, and the Commanding General (CG) of Army Materiel Command (AMC). The research was conducted in the Military Logistics Program of the RAND Arroyo Center, a federally funded research and development center sponsored by the United States Army.

---

[1] The Army changed the name of this initiative to Army Distribution Management (ADM) in January 2003. However, this report retains the VM terminology for contextual consistency.

Contents

Preface... iii

Figures.. vii

Tables... ix

Summary.. xi

Acknowledgments.. xix

Acronyms... xxi

CHAPTER ONE

Introduction.. 1

Identifying the Causes of Army National-Level Backorders............................... 2

Defining, Measuring, and Improving the Army's Reparable-Management Process............ 3

Organization of This Report.. 5

CHAPTER TWO

Understanding the Scope of the Backorder Problem................................... 7

Defining the Order-Fulfillment Process... 7

Metrics to Define the Scope of the BO Problem.. 8

    Extent of the BO-Rate Problem... 8

    Effect of High BO Rates on Customer Wait Times.................................. 13

Summary.. 16

CHAPTER THREE

Understanding the Reparable-Management Process..................................... 17

The Current Reparable-Management Process... 18

Depot-Level Reparable Workload... 21

    Planning for Both Near-Term and Long-Term Needs................................. 21

    Execution of Repair Programs.. 24

Summary.. 26

CHAPTER FOUR
Improving Planning Activities 29
Key Issues in the Current Process for Planning and Execution of PRONs to Repair
        Reparable Items 29
    Uncertainty in Customer Demands on Long-Term Planning Forecasts 29
    Need for Improved Supply-Management Planning and Execution 34
Approaches for Improving Supply-Management Planning and Execution 36
Approaches for Dealing with Uncertain Demand 37
    Frequent Updating of PRON Forecasts to Respond to Changing Demands 38
    Improving Service Level by Increasing Safety Stock 39
    Improving Replenishment Lead Times 40
    Improving Communication About Customer Needs and Requirements 41
Moving from Planning to Execution 42
    Linking Long-Term Planning to Near-Term Execution 42
Conclusion 44

CHAPTER FIVE
Improving Repair Activities 45
Improving Repair-Activity Responsiveness to Deal with Uncertain Demand 45
Approaches for Improving Repair-Activity Responsiveness 46
    Reducing Lead Time for Next-Repair Completion and Overall Repair Flow Time 47
    Frequent Replanning to Keep Repairs Synchronized with Demand 49
    Improving the Availability of Unserviceable Assets 51
    Improving the Process for Managing Repair Parts 53
    Financial Policies That Support More-Responsive Depot Repairs 63
Conclusion 68

CHAPTER SIX
Recommendations for Pilot Implementation 71
The Need for a More-Responsive Reparable-Management Process 71
Recommendations for a Pilot Effort 72
    Addressing Uncertainty 73
    Properly Linking Long-Term Planning and Replanning for Responsive Execution 74
    Improving Repair Responsiveness 76
Conclusion 78

Bibliography 81

Figures

1.1. Key Components of the Define-Measure-Improve Methodology 4
2.1. The Order-Fulfillment Process 8
2.2. BOs Reported for Army Tactical-Level Requisitions to the National System 9
2.3. BO Rates for AMC-Managed Items, by Type of Repair or Consumable 11
2.4. BO Rates at the MSCs Within AMC 12
2.5. Process Flow Diagram for Army Field-Level Customer Requisitions 14
2.6. CWT Statistics for a Mechanized Infantry Division Installation 15
3.1. Key Activities of the Current Reparable-Management Process 18
3.2. Reparable-Management Process Activities to Replenish Serviceable
     Inventories 20
3.3. Supply-Management and Repair Activities of the Reparable-Management
     Process 21
3.4. Tools Used by Item Managers to Understand Demand Patterns (Planning
     Sequence for Repair-Process Program Development by TACOM IM) 22
3.5. Depot-Level Maintenance and Repair Activities 27
4.1. Variability in Demand for the FY2000 Reparable M88A1 30
4.2. The Repair-Planning Processes for Different PRONs 32
4.3. FY2000 M88A1 PRON vs. Actual Demands 33
4.4. The FY2000 M88A1 Engine PRON Revised to Meet Customer Demands 36
4.5. Current Reparable-Management Activities 43
4.6. A More-Responsive Reparable-Management Process 44
5.1. Repair Production at ANAD Under the FY2000 PRON and the Revised
     PRON 46
5.2. Generalized Reverse Logistics Process 52

Tables

2.1. Requisitioning Data for FY2002... 10
5.1. An Example of Current Cost Allocation vs. Marginal Cost Allocation 67

Summary

High Backorder Rates for Reparable Items

Since its inception in 1995, the Army's Velocity Management (VM) initiative, now known as Army Distribution Management (ADM), has been used to improve the responsiveness, reliability, and efficiency of the Army's logistics system. However, as VM efforts expanded from order fulfillment at the tactical-unit level to national-inventory management, a troubling pattern emerged: a multiyear pattern of high and variable backorder (BO) rates for reparable items managed by the Army Materiel Command (AMC) and all the major subordinate commands (MSCs) within AMC.

A reparable is an item that can be cost-effectively repaired. When a reparable such as a diesel engine or turbine fuel control malfunctions, it can be replaced by a repaired or rebuilt component; it usually does not need to be replaced by a new item.

From the perspective of the ultimate customer—an Army mechanic trying to bring a malfunctioning piece of equipment back to mission-capable status—a BO can mean a lengthy delay and potentially a shortfall in mission support. The pattern of high BO rates suggests that improvements are needed in the process for managing and repairing reparable items. Improved effectiveness and efficiency of AMC's component-repair capabilities and capacity can also contribute directly to other depot programs (e.g., components are also used to repair higher reparable assemblies and even for end-item overhauls), in addition to returning serviceable assets to the shelf, where they will be available for issue to those Army customers directly responsible for repairing mission equipment.

To illustrate the process-improvement approach described in this report, we use a case study of the M88A1 armored recovery vehicle engine. This diesel engine, which has had persistent BO problems, is typical of a large group of unsophisticated, older components needed to keep aging weapon systems in mission-ready condition.

Planning and Execution of the Reparable-Management Process

When an end-item fault or malfunction is discovered, during either equipment operation or routine maintenance, if a serviceable reparable is needed to complete the end-item repair, a mechanic requests the part or component from the supply system. The reparable-management process begins with the identification of the malfunctioning component and ends when a serviceable asset is made available through either repair or vendor replenishment to replace the item issued to the mechanic.

Whether or not there are serviceable reparables in stock at the national level depends on the effectiveness and responsiveness of the AMC process for planning and executing reparable workload, both repair programs and new buys. The planning activity analyzes inventory levels and produces a formal decision package for a reparable repair program or a vendor procurement, both known as a PRON (procurement-request order number) that is submitted for approval. Over the long term, the planning process also provides input to the Army working-capital fund (AWCF) budget process and the program-objective memorandum (POM) budget planning process, which has a rolling six-year planning horizon and ultimately feeds into the congressional appropriations process.

Once a repair PRON receives management approval, it is typically scheduled to begin execution at the start of a new fiscal year 18 months after the start of the planning cycle. Once a repair is completed, the item manager (IM) may immediately ship the item to a customer to satisfy a due out, move it to a centralized distribution depot for future issue, or leave it in storage at the distribution center collocated with the repair facility.

The PRON is usually described as a yearly repair requirement. Unserviceable items are often inducted in monthly batches, and output is also usually processed in batches. However, the formal PRON process also drives the overall planning process for long-term capacity adjustments (e.g., workforce, equipment, facilities). Quarterly replanning meetings provide a venue for adjusting production schedules.

Three Critical Issues in the Reparable-Management Process

Our examination of the reparable-management process identified three key issues that need to be addressed:

- The impact of uncertainty and variability in customer demands on long-term planning forecasts.
- The need for increased emphasis on near-term replanning for execution.
- The inability of repair responsiveness to meet changing requirements.

The Impact of Uncertainty and Variability in Customer Demands on Long-Term Planning Forecasts

The current process for planning reparable workload requires and uses forecasts made over long horizons. It is nearly impossible to accurately make such forecasts 18 to 30 months into the future because of changes in mission scenarios and other sources of demand uncertainty and demand variability. In other words, forecast error is to be expected.

We use the M88A1 diesel engine to illustrate a case in which increasing demand over the extended planning horizon led to underproduction. In this example, forecast error was caused by demand uncertainty, rather than variability. The current planning process can also create the opposite situation by overproducing items with declining demand. In either case, the reparable-management process must be capable of adapting to changing demand. Fundamentally, successful planning requires frequent replanning to incorporate emerging information so that the execution will meet valid needs.

Increased Emphasis on Near-Term Replanning for Execution

The reparable-management process tends to focus primarily on long-term budget planning, and thus it is less responsive to changing customer needs that emerge during near-term execution. Although the MSCs and their repair depots hold quarterly meetings to revise schedules and address problem areas, these meetings typically focus on only the most critical issues.

Improved Repair Responsiveness to Meet Changing Requirements

To the extent that an IM can change a production plan or program to meet changing demands, the question arises as to whether the depot can adjust its repair program to meet those changing demands. We found, for example, that the procedures used for inventory management and control at Anniston Army Depot (ANAD) did not provide sufficient visibility to identify repair-part problems before they became critical in the production process.[2]

Alternatives for Improving the Reparable-Planning Process

Strategies for Dealing with Uncertain Demand

A review of the literature on commercial business practices identified the following four promising approaches for meeting customer needs under conditions of uncertain demand:

---

[2] The case study provided an in-depth view of ANAD, but similar systems and policies would have similar results at other Army depots with similar workloads.

- Frequently update forecasts.
- Increase safety stock.
- Improve replenishment lead times.
- Improve communication about customer needs and requirements.

Frequently update forecasts. The literature suggests that the fundamental problem in forecasting reparable demand is not the type of model used but the length of the planning horizon. Some decisions must be made with the best information available at the time, whereas other decisions can be revisited as new information emerges. The forecasting model used in the reparable-management process is capable of making adjustments. In planning a repair program, an IM uses several tools, including the Requirements Determination and Execution System (RD&ES), which analyzes data on demands and other transactions in order to make recommendations for repair and/or buy quantities. RD&ES generates a monthly repair plan that starts with an updated forecast (using an exponential moving average model) supplemented by known factors that have changed or are expected to change, such as fielded equipment density, operating tempo, etc. This approach can rapidly adjust to changing conditions, helping accommodate highly variable demand. Forecasting for PRON execution and production control could be improved through frequent recalculations to update predictions with current data. The near-term predictions we reviewed during the case study demonstrated improved output.

Increase safety stock. Safety stock refers to inventory that is held to buffer a process against uncertainty. The RD&ES module has the capability to determine safety-stock needs within the planning calculation. Safety stock should not be considered merely an added cost to the logistics system.

Improve replenishment lead times. The time to process and deliver a customer order for a component or part is known as the lead time. If a request for an item can be filled immediately from tactical- or national-level inventory, the lead time can be very short, but when the request cannot be satisfied until the next repair is completed, the lead time can be quite long. In the case of the M88A1 engine, the lead time necessary to fill a customer request might be many days or weeks if the reparable is not in stock, mostly due to lengthy queuing or waiting times within the various depot repair activities.

Approaches to reducing lead time must examine the chain of events necessary to meet a need to determine where it is more efficient and effective to insert buffers or to reduce constraints so that the desired response time can be achieved at lower total cost. It is possible, for example, that some work-in-process (WIP) engines could be used to shorten the achievable repair time. All the activities in the chain of lead-time events should be addressed to improve responsiveness.

Improve communication about customer needs and requirements. The pattern of changing customer demands for reparables is not likely to change. In light of such realities, it is important to adjust expectations and to increase communication about how the process must change to better meet customer needs and requirements. Customers and providers across the system supported by the Army's reparable-management process must understand both the nature of the issues involved and actions that could contribute to an improved outcome. Unless the process changes, the outcome is not likely to change.

Frequent Replanning and Near-Term Repair Execution

When the results of the planning process are shown to be inadequate to meet emerging customer demand, the plans should be adjusted promptly under appropriate management controls. An initial goal might be to transition as quickly as possible to monthly repair-schedule changes (i.e., replanning) using the available monthly RD&ES outputs. In the future, the management decision process might be informed weekly or even daily about customer demand, and production-schedule changes could be implemented when warranted.

Improving Repair Responsiveness

Several alternatives for improving repair responsiveness emerged from interactions with managers and technicians within the system and from lessons learned from commercial practice.

Reduce lead time for the next repair and overall repair flow time. Reducing flow time in the repair activities of the reparable-management process will involve looking very closely at all the process activities required to return a broken asset to serviceable status and to deliver it to the Defense Logistics Agency (DLA) distribution center packaged and ready for issue. The intent of such analysis would be to establish a mechanism that could respond to customer needs by increasing production when demand increases, thus reducing the potential for BOs, and decreasing production when demand is low, thus reducing unnecessary inventory investment.

Replan frequently to synchronize repairs with demand. Updated information could be used monthly by the current RD&ES module to revise production schedules that cover the currently approved PRONs. In addition, the proposed lead-time reduction efforts could provide the kinds of operating practices necessary to enable depot production to respond to forecast changes. A mechanism or signal should be established that communicates to depot managers and workers the need to perform a given task and the quantity of items to be produced. This replanning works two ways: It *increases* production when demand increases, thus reducing the potential for BOs, and it *decreases* production when demands are not as great as forecasted, thus reducing unnecessary inventory investment.

Assure the availability of unserviceable assets. Repair actions cannot begin until unserviceable assets that have been removed from end-items are available for induction. Currently, unserviceables (unless they are specially identified) are treated as the lowest-priority items within both the supply and the transportation activities. The supply and transportation communities need to review the priorities assigned to dealing with unserviceable assets to allow them to be used more effectively in meeting the needs of individual customers and the Army as a whole.

Improve the process for managing depot repair parts. Under the current process, technicians must leave their work locations and go to the shop supply room to get parts that are needed, wasting time and manpower. A more effective approach would be to provide repair parts, both new and reclaimed (i.e., recycled), at the workstations. For example, routing reclaimed parts to the Automated Storage and Retrieval System (ASRS) facility would improve visibility of assets and would allow parts to be brought forward to mechanics in an orderly manner.

The inventory policy for repair parts at AMC maintenance depots would also benefit from greater flexibility in setting inventory levels for different items. Current policy sets inventory levels at 60 days of supply (DOS) for all items other than bench stock and special-project assets. A more flexible policy would allow for addressing the different characteristics of individual repair parts, thus reducing the risk of stockouts. Such a policy might distinguish among at least three kinds of items:

- **Items used for nearly all repairs.** As long as there is recurring monthly production or availability of these items, replenishment with the current 60-DOS policy should ensure that assets are on hand and that there is a continuing vendor relationship to meet future needs. Over time, the 60-DOS level might actually be reduced. For these types of items, replenishment time and variability, as well as cost, should determine the final inventory depth.
- **Less frequently used items.** The programmed logic for inventory decisions in DLA's automated inventory-replenishment system is based on the frequency with which items are ordered. Low-demand items replenished by large orders are typically replenished only infrequently and thus may not be stocked at DLA if the repair depot orders them too infrequently to qualify them for stockage. Infrequent orders also complicate vendor relationships. Smaller, more-frequent replacement orders have the benefit of both limiting inventory investment and communicating to IMs and vendors the continuing need for such items to support repair programs. The relevant IMs must understand that these less frequently used items are still necessary.
- **Infrequently used items with long lead times for replenishment.** These items require and justify intensive management. They typically represent a small percentage of the total number of items but a majority of the total inventory investment.

Adopt policies that make repair programs responsive to customer demands. The Army maintenance depots' component-repair programs are financed via the

AWCF, which does not require that revolving-fund activities spend all their funds by the end of the fiscal year to avoid losing the money. Thus, a depot can carry over workload beyond its intended fiscal year to provide approved cash flow for labor and materiel while awaiting the approval of a new PRON. Workload carryover and the pattern of delayed production, along with changes in demand, contribute to the due-out volume, or the BO rate. The Army needs a policy that is more responsive to customer demands.

Adopt financial policies that encourage appropriate use of repair capacity. Prices of Army-managed items include a supply-management surcharge to recover the costs of operating the national supply system. This surcharge, which includes both fixed costs (costs that do not vary by supply-management activity) and variable costs (costs generated by specific items), can result in comparatively high prices and can lead to lost sales—even for items with low acquisition costs. For example, the surcharge acts as a "tax" on purchases from the supply system, whereas locally purchased or repaired equivalents avoid such a charge. One approach for addressing this problem would be to fund fixed costs (e.g., costs for Department of Defense (DoD) agencies, depreciation, and adjustments for prior-year losses or gains) through direct funding and to allocate variable costs more specifically to the items generating them.

A Pilot Effort to Implement Improvements

The implementation of improvement initiatives can be made more tractable by starting with a pilot effort that allows the development and testing of alternative approaches. The results obtained in a pilot implementation could be measured, rules could be adjusted, and confidence would be developed in the selected improvement approaches.

We recommend that senior management at an MSC appoint a small pilot implementation team. The team's effort should focus initially upon a few reparable NIINs (national item identification numbers) related to a single weapon system or end-item that is repaired at the same facility. This approach could create a vertical slice of the overall reparable-management process and thus would facilitate actions across activities to achieve recognized results.

It is possible to dramatically improve the availability of reparables to customers. This report discusses approaches that can efficiently improve each activity in the process. Many of these approaches are drawn from successful commercial practice, and others derive from successes within military practice that deserve expansion.

Acknowledgments

The authors wish to thank the many people who have helped to make this research possible. We first thank General John Coburn (USA, Ret) for his support, initially as Deputy Chief of Staff for Logistics (G4), HQDA, and then as Commanding General (CG) of Army Materiel Command (AMC). We are also indebted to LTG Charles Mahan (USA, Ret) for his support in his roles as Deputy CG of AMC and then as the Army G4. Thanks also go to Eric Orsini, the Special Assistant to the Army G4 (and then Deputy Assistant Secretary of the Army for Logistics), and his associates, COL Glenn Harrold and COL Albert Love. At AMC Headquarters, we thank General Paul Kern, Commanding General; MG Mitchell Stevenson, Deputy Chief of Staff, G3; COL Hugh Hudson; and Thomas Hedstrom. At AMC's Tank-Automotive and Armaments Command (TACOM) we thank MG N. Ross Thompson, Commanding General, and Thomas Boyle, David Carter, Chris Thomasson, and John Jacobs. At the Anniston Army Depot (ANAD), we thank Borden Norten, David Sok, and Shelby Cupp. Thanks also to the many other dedicated Army, AMC, and Combined Arms Support Command (CASCOM) staff who provided assistance.

The research reported here follows directly from earlier RAND Velocity Management (VM) research for the Army Deputy Chief of Staff, G4. We are indebted to LTG Claude Christianson, Army G4, and Thomas Edwards, Deputy to the Commander, CASCOM, and Executive Agent for Army Distribution Management, for their continued interest in research aimed at improving support to Army warfighters and at implementing change to improve Army logistics processes.

RAND research explicitly addressing the impacts of the uncertainty of logistics requirements and the implicit requirement for process changes to create more responsive capabilities, including responsive repair, improved distribution, and the application of "lean" management concepts, can be traced at least to the late 1970s. RAND colleagues including Irv K. Cohen, Gordon B. Crawford, and James S. Hodges created a body of work that bibliographic references only begin to document.

We are grateful for the efforts of two formal reviewers who contributed directly to the clarity and quality of this report. Vincent Mabert of Indiana University and

Lionel Galway of RAND made substantive, direct contributions that improved the quality of our research.

At RAND, we wish to thank Eric Peltz, John Dumond, Rick Eden, Marc Robbins, Ken Girardini, Chris Hanks, and Patricia Boren for their contributions to this document and for providing feedback as the project progressed. Kristin Leuschner provided fundamental guidance and excellent prose that vastly improved the report. Finally, thanks go to Sarita M. Anderson for formatting the draft of this document and managing its preparation.

Acronyms

ADM	Army Distribution Management
AMC	Army Materiel Command
AMCOM	Aviation and Missile Command
AMDF	Army Master Data File
ANAD	Anniston Army Depot
APICS	American Production and Inventory Control Society
AR	Army regulation
ASL	authorized stockage list
ASRS	Automated Storage and Retrieval System
AWCF	Army working-capital fund
BO	backorder
CASCOM	United States Army Combined Arms Support Command
CCP	containerization and consolidation point
CCSS	Commodity Command Standard System
CECOM	Communications and Electronics Command
CFS	container freight station
CG	Commanding General
Class IX	repair parts, class of supplies
CLM	Council of Logistics Management
CONUS	Continental United States
CTASC	Corps Theater Automatic Data Processing Service Center
CWT	customer wait time
DAAS	Defense Automated Addressing System
DAASC	Defense Automated Addressing System Center
DDJC	Defense Distribution Depot, San Joaquin, California

DDSP	Defense Distribution Depot, Susquehanna, Pennsylvania
DLA	Defense Logistics Agency
DLR	depot-level reparable
DM	Distribution Management
DMI	define, measure, improve
DMWR	depot-maintenance work requirement
DoD	Department of Defense
DOS	days of supply
DRMS	Defense Reutilization and Marketing Service
DVD	direct vendor delivery
DWCF	Defense working-capital fund
FDP	forward distribution point
FLR	field-level reparable
FMR	Financial Management Regulation
FMS	foreign military sales
G4	Deputy Chief of Staff for Logistics
GAO	General Accounting Office
GSA	General Services Administration
HQ	headquarters
ICP	inventory control point
ILAP	Integrated Logistics Analysis Program
IM	item manager
ISA	installation supply account
IT	information technology
LAC	latest acquisition cost
LIDB	Logistics Information Data Base
LIF	Logistics Information File
LMP	Logistics Modernization Program
LORA	level-of-repair analysis
M88A1	armored recovery vehicle; type, model designation
MRO	materiel release order
MSC	major subordinate command (of AMC)
MTBF	mean time between failure

NICP	national inventory-control point
NIIN	national item identification number
NMWR	national maintenance work requirement
NRTS	not repairable this station
NSN	national stock number
OCONUS	overseas, outside the Continental United States
OMA	Operations and Maintenance, Army
OMB	Office of Management and Budget
OSD	Office of the Secretary of Defense
PEP	parts-explosion process
POD	point of debarcation
POE	point of embarcation
POM	program-objective memorandum
PPBS	Planning, Programming, and Budgeting System
PRON	procurement-request order number
RD&ES	Requirements Determination and Execution System
RPAS	Repair and Procurement Acquisition System
SAMS	Standard Army Maintenance System
SARSS	Standard Army Retail Supply System
SDP	strategic distribution platform
SLE	service-life extension
SOR	source of repair
SSA	supply support activity
SSF	Single Stock Fund
TACOM	Tank–Automotive and Armaments Command
ULLS	Unit-Level Logistics System
USA	United States Army
USC	United States Code
VM	Velocity Management
WIP	work in process

CHAPTER ONE

Introduction

Since its inception in 1995, the Army's Velocity Management (VM) initiative[1] has sought to improve the responsiveness, reliability, and efficiency of the Army's logistics system. By implementing a simple, yet powerful, process-improvement methodology, the Army has dramatically streamlined its order-fulfillment process, i.e., the supply and the distribution activities that meet its customers' needs. VM has enabled the Army to cut median order-fulfillment times for spare parts and materiel by nearly two-thirds across installations in the continental United states (CONUS) and by over 75 percent at several major installations.[2]

Initially, VM was applied only to the distribution of available inventory assets. However, efforts soon turned to the problem of improving the availability of those assets. As the VM stream of research and analysis expanded from order fulfillment at the tactical-unit level into efforts to improve national-inventory management, the analysis exposed a troubling pattern: Wholesale backorders (BOs) were higher than expected.[3]

Wholesale BOs had been masked by the slowness of the previous overall order-fulfillment process. Every segment of that process, BO and non-BO alike, took a long time. The improvements in responsiveness of the process exposed the glaring impact of BOs on total sustainment performance. VM's overall responsiveness metric (i.e., customer wait time (CWT)) established an improved foundation for measuring basic logistics processes. As a process improves, the expected evolution is sequential exposure of the next area in need of improvement. Indeed, as the order-fulfillment process improved, the contribution or impact of the BO issues became more clearly

---

[1] In 2003, VM was renamed Army Distribution Management (ADM). In this report, we have retained the VM terminology for contextual consistency

[2] To learn more about the VM program, see Dumond, Brauner, Eden, et al., 2001; Dumond, Eden, and Folkeson, 1995; and Wang, 2000.

[3] A wholesale BO occurs when a requisition is passed to the national level for "wholesale" fulfillment and cannot be immediately satisfied from on-hand inventory. Direct vendor deliveries (DVDs) can also experience BOs when materiel is not provided in accordance with contract parameters.

defined and exposed. The process-improvement approach described in this report attempts to understand the causes of the exposed issues.[4]

Identifying the Causes of Army National-Level Backorders

Inventory planning recognizes the presence of demand variability, and current Army supply policy calls for providing an 85 percent service level (i.e., on average, customers should encounter no more than a 15 percent BO rate). Given variability in both demand and replenishment lead time, inventory levels—specifically safety levels and order-quantity combinations—are set to have parts in stock 85 percent of the time.[5] When the BO trend exceeds 15 percent, either inventory investment did not occur as planned, planning is not being executed promptly, demand is being underforecast, or process performance (i.e., procurement lead time or repair lead time) is not in line with planning parameters.[6]

An item of supply is generally categorized as either consumable or reparable. A consumable is normally expended or used up beyond economic recovery during its intended period of use. A reparable is an item that can be cost-effectively repaired, such as a diesel engine or turbine fuel control. When a reparable malfunctions, it can usually be replaced by a repaired or rebuilt component rather than requiring replacement by a new item.[7] In fact, repaired or rebuilt parts are sometimes the only source of stock for expensive weapon-system components. Usually, reparables are repaired to serviceable condition for subsequent reissue to customers. (Throughout this report, the term *reparable* is used to refer to a class of items; individual reparables may be deemed either repairable or unrepairable.[8]) However, some unserviceable reparables, after inspection, are deemed to be unrepairable at a particular repair location or may even be condemned as economically unrepairable or infeasible to repair.

When we examined Army field-level customer-satisfaction statistics, we discovered that the high BO rate was being driven by a BO rate for reparables higher than

---

[4] The issue of BOs was also raised by Congress, resulting in requests for the General Accounting Office (GAO) to look into the matter. GAO has addressed this and other issues related to the Army and other Department of Defense (DoD) entities in an extensive list of publications. For example, see GAO, 1990a, 1993, 2001a.

[5] This is an aggregate target. Different parts have different targets, based upon the most cost-effective allocation of assets to achieve the overall goal.

[6] Delays associated with vendor replenishments or wholesale inventories can involve a complex set of issues and processes.

[7] The term *reparable* correctly refers to both new items procured from a vendor and repaired items. Inventory of a specific reparable may include both new and repaired items. However, some items become so worn or damaged that they can no longer be economically repaired and are thus condemned and disposed of.

[8] Reparable items include depot-level reparables (DLR) and field-level reparables (FLR), categorized by the authorized level of repair, which depends upon the skills, tools, and equipment required.

that for consumables. We found a multiyear trend of high BO rates for reparable items managed by Army Materiel Command (AMC),[9] a pattern that also applied to all the major subordinate commands (MSCs) within AMC. The problem was not simply one of insufficient repairs or procurements—according to the GAO, some items were repaired in insufficient numbers, while others were repaired in excess of computed stock levels.[10]

Defining, Measuring, and Improving the Army's Reparable-Management Process

Distribution Management (DM), the Army's initiative for improving the speed and accuracy of Army logistics processes, employs a systematic methodology for process improvement. As the original name *Velocity Management* implies, the initiative seeks to satisfy the support needs of customers by improving the agility and responsiveness of logistics processes. Under VM/DM, both information and materiel flow faster and more accurately, and at a lower total cost.

To implement DM, the Army has institutionalized a methodology consisting of three steps: define the process, measure the process, and improve the process (DMI). The key components of these steps are summarized in Figure 1.1.[11]

This study addresses the need for improvement of the Army's reparable-management process within AMC.[12] It embraces the spirit of the VM methodology in that it attempts to define this process in detail. However, our ability to measure the process was limited by data availability; we therefore focus on improvement alternatives for a case study of one selected item.[13]

---

[9] The evidence of BOs will be discussed further in Chapter Two.

[10] For many years, Congress has had a continuing interest in improving the management of reparable spares and the inventory of resulting serviceables. The GAO was tasked by Congress on numerous occasions with auditing and/or analyzing various issues related to the management and operation of the military's repair depots. Whether the specific management environment under review was appropriations or revolving funds, the thread of continuity across the observations reported was the need to make each type of decision based on the most recent data available. See, for example, GAO, 1990b.

[11] For more information on the development of VM, see Dumond, Brauner, Eden, et al., 2001.

[12] Unfortunately, because of the inherent variability in demand for weapon-system spare parts, an "optimal" solution that yields zero BOs is not a realistic objective. Although the variability phenomenon has been studied for many years, no successful strategies have been found to control either the demand or the supply variability in practice. See, for example, Crawford, 1988. One of the objectives of the research described in the present report is to identify potential initiatives aimed at reducing supply variability through improvement of the reparable-management process.

[13] This initial effort focused on the Tank–Automotive and Armaments Command (TACOM) and its primary maintenance depot, Anniston Army Depot (ANAD). The data collection and field visits occurred during FY2000.

Figure 1.1
Key Components of the Define-Measure-Improve Methodology

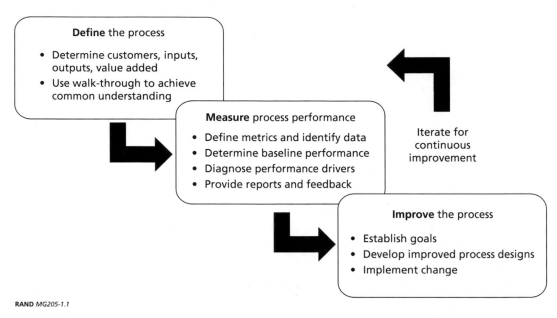

Define the process

- Determine customers, inputs, outputs, value added
- Use walk-through to achieve common understanding

Measure process performance

- Define metrics and identify data
- Determine baseline performance
- Diagnose performance drivers
- Provide reports and feedback

Iterate for continuous improvement

Improve the process

- Establish goals
- Develop improved process designs
- Implement change

RAND *MG205-1.1*

We have not attempted to address the overall improvement of depot maintenance per se. The depot component-repair workload is not the largest part of the depot maintenance workload, in terms of either man-hours or budget. However, component-repair capabilities and capacity are essential for executing the larger overhaul and recapitalization workloads and for direct support to warfighters. Thus, not only will improved effectiveness and efficiency in component repairs return serviceable assets to the shelf, where they will be available to issue to Army customers, it will also contribute directly to other depot programs. In addition, these improvements should improve overall supply system efficiency by reducing overproduction of serviceables and other unnecessary resource investments.

Our goal is to suggest an improvement path for the reparable-management process, based on the evidence uncovered during the case study and driven by relevant critical metrics. Our case study focuses on the M88A1 armored recovery vehicle engine.[14] This engine, which has experienced persistent BO problems, is typical of a large group of unsophisticated, older components that are needed to keep the long-lived current weapon systems in mission-ready condition. The alternatives examined in this study call for added resource investment (e.g., increased safety stock) to buffer the customer from the processes that are not responding rapidly enough. The assumptions behind a continuous-process-improvement strategy recognize that change

---

[14] This 10-cylinder, turbo-charged diesel engine (national stock number (NSN) 2815-00-124-5387) has 1,790 cu in. displacement and comes with all accessories installed.

will occur over time and that intermediate states throughout the transition to the desired state may require some "targeted" investment or infusions of capital. However, these investments will likely provide better service at the same or lower total cost to the Army.

This analysis was undertaken with the knowledge that a logistics-systems modernization effort is under way to improve decision support in both the supply and maintenance management areas. Furthermore, AMC has undertaken an effort to improve depot maintenance through the application of "lean" manufacturing concepts at each of its depots.[15] Our analysis specifically addresses improvement opportunities that need not await technological modernization, nor do they conflict with it. Furthermore, the recommendations presented here are totally congruent with a "lean" view of both the planning and execution of the reparable-management process.

Organization of This Report

The remainder of the report is organized into five chapters. Chapter Two takes a closer look at the nature of the problems associated with a high BO rate. Chapter Three examines the current reparable-management process and identifies some key issues that need to be addressed within that process. Chapters Four and Five offer solution alternatives relevant to inventory planning and repair management, respectively. Chapter Six summarizes the recommendations for improving the reparable-management process.

---

[15] See Chapter Five for a more detailed discussion of lean manufacturing.

CHAPTER TWO

Understanding the Scope of the Backorder Problem

In this chapter, we employ a suite of metrics to examine the issues involved in reparable-inventory planning and repair activities. We first define the order-fulfillment process, which is delayed by BOs, and we then introduce metrics to measure the effects of those BOs. The metrics measure not only the BO rate (the proportion of requisitions that became BOs), but also the impact of high BO rates on overall performance, i.e., responsiveness to customer requisitions.

Defining the Order-Fulfillment Process

Define, the first step of the VM process-improvement methodology, produces a clear picture of the process (common to all participants and stakeholders) through process mapping. Figure 2.1 illustrates the Army's order-fulfillment process for spare parts and related materiel needed by equipment mechanics, the ultimate customer in this example. Within the figure, solid lines represent materiel flows, and dashed lines represent information flows.

The customer (shown on the left) diagnoses an equipment fault and initiates a request for a part, which can be filled either by one of the installation's tactical (retail) supply activities or by the national-level (wholesale) supply system. When the request for a part cannot be met locally, the national-level supply manager passes the requisition on to the appropriate source for fulfillment. In the case of a reparable, the requisition would go to a national distribution center, which would supply the part. If no reparable items are currently available to fill the request, a BO or due-out is generated, and BO status information is passed to the supply activity supporting the customer. Eventually, the customer's request is satisfied by either a repaired serviceable or a new asset.

Figure 2.1
The Order-Fulfillment Process

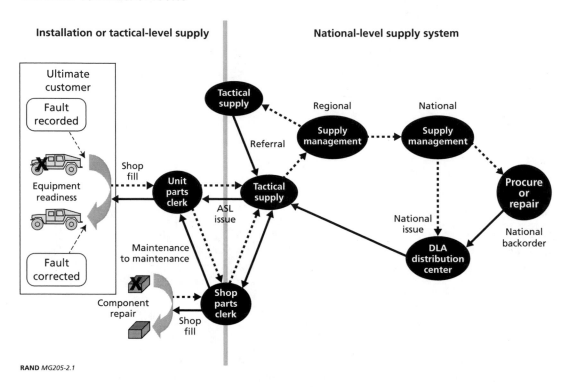

RAND *MG205-2.1*

Metrics to Define the Scope of the BO Problem

Following the VM philosophy, we chose metrics that reflect the perspective of the ultimate customers and their supply activity or forward distribution point (FDP), formerly known as the supply support activity (SSA). These metrics—BO rate, customer wait time (CWT), and workaround rate—all relate to the responsiveness and effectiveness of the supply chain.[1]

Extent of the BO-Rate Problem

We began our research by measuring confirmed BO status recorded in the customers' Standard Army Retail Supply System (SARSS) and archived in the Corps Theater

---

[1] The metrics used in such process-improvement efforts are not necessarily the same metrics reported elsewhere within the Army logistics system. These "new" metrics tend to evolve as the improvement efforts that use them evolve and need measurement better aligned with customer needs and process diagnosis.

The BOs reported here represent a total composite statistic that includes those for requests by the ultimate Army customer and those for field-level supply-activity replenishment. The reported statistics do not include BOs for other requesters (e.g., depot-level maintenance requests).

Automatic Data Processing Service Center (CTASC) document history files.[2] The extent of the BO problem can be seen in Figure 2.2, which displays five years of BO rates for spare parts (supply Class IX items), sorted by national agencies that manage different sets of these items.[3] During this period, the BO rate for AMC-managed items was higher than that for items managed by the Defense Logistics Agency (DLA) and the General Services Administration (GSA).[4]

The BO rate, or percentage, was calculated by dividing the number of BO requisitions (i.e., requisitions with "BB" status according to the item manager) by the total number of requisitions for the same period. Only requisitions for spare parts are

Figure 2.2
BOs Reported for Army Tactical-Level Requisitions to the National System

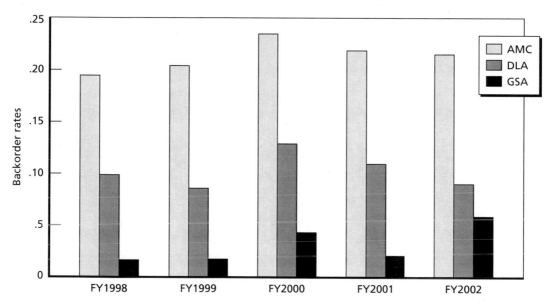

SOURCE: Army LIDB data, Class IX BO rates for closed requisitions, CONUS and OCONUS active units, no DVDs.
RAND *MG205-2.2*

---

[2] Backorders are indicated by a supply-status code of "BB."

[3] The BO rate is calculated based on all spare-part requisitions by active Army retail customers (i.e., BO requisitions/total requisitions). Rates are calculated based on requisitions, not NIINs (national item identification numbers). The Army sorts all NIINs into ten separate categories. The spare parts used in our calculations are in the Class IX category.

[4] The items ordered by Army customers have inventory-management processes performed by AMC, the Defense Logistics Agency (DLA), or the General Services Administration (GSA). DLA tends to manage more-common items used by more than one service or agency, while AMC tends to manage specialized and weapon-system-unique items for the Army. Reparables tend to be managed by AMC. The DLA-managed items also tend to cost less than the AMC-managed items. Those GSA-managed items are generally paper and housekeeping-type items, but they also include a small number of consumable items in support of repairs.

included. This metric does not consider the duration of the due-out status or the time required to fill the customer's request. It merely reflects the proportion of BO occurrences.

The BO rates in Figure 2.2 do not correspond to those computed internally by the individual agencies. Each agency has slightly different definitions of BO rates, based on the factors under its control.

Table 2.1 provides some added perspective on the data summarized in Figure 2.2. The table shows the population of requisitions by tactical-level Army active-duty customers. These are requisitions for spare parts that were delivered to customers during FY2002. The data are sorted by the wholesale agency that manages a NIIN (national item identification number), and by whether that NIIN is a reparable or a consumable.[5] The italicized percentage values are to be read horizontally (e.g., 84.3 percent of the total requisitions are for DLA-managed items), and the values in bold type are to be read vertically (e.g., 95.2 percent of the requisitions for DLA-managed items are for consumables).

A 15 percent BO rate is the expected result of current Army inventory policy, and it is the goal in the annual Army working -capital fund (AWCF) budget process; the supply managers (in AMC) and their models thus compute inventory levels using an 85 percent supply-availability goal ($1.0 - 0.85 = 0.15$). However, although the 85 percent availability factor is incorporated into numerous policies and algorithms, we have not found the source of this specific goal in law, written policy, or regulation

Table 2.1
Requisitioning Data for FY2002

FY2002	AMC	DLA	GSA	Total
NIINs requisitioned	22,365 (*11.1%*)	178,312 (*88.8%*)	160 (*0.08%*)	200,837
Reparable	15,154 (*40.3%*) (**68%**)	22,378 (*59.6%*) (**13%**)	14 (*0.01%*) (**9%**)	37,546 (**18.7%**)
Consumable	7,211 (*4.4%*) (**32%**)	155,934 (*95.5%*) (**87%**)	146 (*0.1%*) (**91%**)	163,291 (**81.3%**)
Total requisitions	824,824 (*15.4%*)	4,503,093 (*84.3%*)	15,543 (*0.3%*)	5,343,460
Reparable	481,514 (*69.1%*) (**58.4%**)	215,179 (*30.8%*) (**4.8%**)	112 (*0.02%*) (**0.7%**)	696,805 (**13%**)
Consumable	343,310 (*7.4%*) (**41.6%**)	4,287,914 (*92.3%*) (**95.2%**)	15,431 (*0.3%*) (**99.3%**)	4,646,655 (**87%**)
BO requisitions	177,528	405,371	911	583,810
Reparable	115,632	35,816	3	151,451
Consumable	61,896	369,555	908	432,359
BO rate	**21.5%**	**9.0%**	**5.9%**	**10.9%**
Reparable	**24.0%**	**16.6%**	**2.7%**	**21.7%**
Consumable	**18.0%**	**8.6%**	**5.9%**	**9.3%**

SOURCE: LIDB, Class IX, CONUS and OCONUS (overseas, outside the CONUS) active units, no DVDs.

---

[5] In this case, a reparable could be either a field-level or depot-level item, depending on the applicable maintenance-recovery code.

within the Army or the Office of the Secretary of Defense (OSD). DLA is not using the same policy and has exceeded the 85 percent supply-availability goal significantly, both overall and for consumable items, to the benefit of Army customers in FY2002. Regardless, inventory-policy levels should be set on the basis of desired customer mission-support capabilities, considering the conditions of logistics responsiveness, demand predictability, acceptable risk, and acceptable cost.[6]

As shown in Figure 2.3, BO rates have been problematic for all categories of AMC-managed items, including depot-level and field-level reparables, as well as consumables.[7] A depot-level reparable (DLR) is designated for repair or disposal at the depot level of maintenance (or is designated for repair below the depot level, but if repair cannot be accomplished at that level, shall have its unserviceable carcass for-

Figure 2.3
BO Rates for AMC-Managed Items, by Type of Repair or Consumable

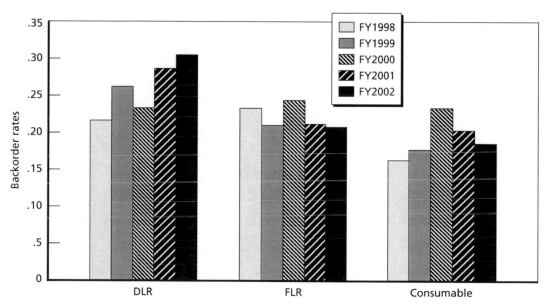

SOURCE: Army CTASC and LIF/LIDB, all AMC Class IX wholesale sales, CONUS and OCONUS active units, no DVDs.
RAND *MG205-2.3*

---

[6] In recent years, the 85 percent supply-availability goal has been discussed in terms of the financial constraints associated with reduced budget levels. However, this goal has been a consistent constraint value in the Pentagon for at least the last 40 years. At any rate, the BO rates for AMC-managed materiel (as measured from the tactical Army customer's perspective over this five-year period) exceeded 15 percent each year.

[7] Since this research began, the Army archive for such data has migrated from the Logistics Information File (LIF) to the Logistics Information Data Base (LIDB).

warded to the depot for repair or condemnation, or reported to the IM for disposition).[8] The technical complexity and equipment necessary to complete the repair determines the level of repair designated. A field-level reparable (FLR) is designated for repair or disposal below the depot level of maintenance. A consumable item is one that is replaced by a new item at the end of its service life, when it is used up beyond the level of economically viable repair. As shown in Figure 2.3, BO rates for all three categories of AMC-managed items exceed the 15 percent BO standard, with the DLR BO rate reaching 30 percent.

Moreover, BO rates are high across all three major subordinate commands (MSCs) within AMC, as shown in Figure 2.4.[9] The figure shows overall AMC BO

Figure 2.4
BO Rates at the MSCs Within AMC

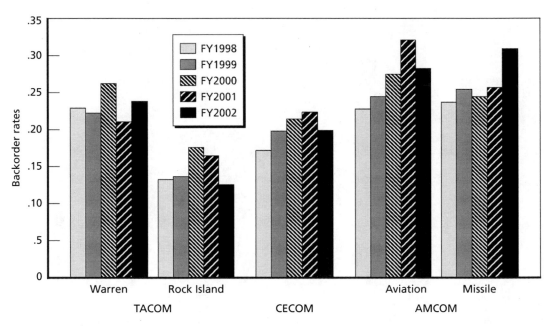

SOURCE: Army CTASC and LIF/LIDB, all AMC Class IX wholesale sales, CONUS and OCONUS active units.
RAND MG205-2.4

---

[8] See Department of Defense, 1995, for definitions.

[9] The BO rates are considered high here because they exceed the Army's target goals. Also, the customers reported BOs as a problem during the VM initiative. More-recent RAND Arroyo Center research (unpublished) by Eric Peltz and Thomas Held benchmarked commercial fleet metrics for the retail and tactical levels and found both the target goals and the performance achieved to be typically well above the 85 percent target. At the same time, the Army's performance does not appear to be significantly worse than that of the other military services.

data across the MSCs, with Tank–Automotive and Armaments Command (TACOM) items further split among management activities at Warren, Michigan, and Rock Island, Illinois; and Aviation and Missile Command (AMCOM) items segregated into aviation and missile, both managed at Huntsville, Alabama. Communications and Electronics Command (CECOM) is at Ft. Monmouth, New Jersey. As shown, AMCOM has the highest rates. CECOM's BO rate was just above the 15 percent level at the beginning of the period but has increased. BOs at TACOM Warren exceeded 20 percent throughout the period, peaking at over 26 percent. Rock Island had the best performance, yet its BO rate exceeded 15 percent in two of the five years. The data indicate that each of the MSCs has had problems consistently meeting the 15 percent BO rate goal.[10]

Effect of High BO Rates on Customer Wait Times

BOs affect customers, who must either delay needed repairs or resort to workarounds when a part is not available. The CWT metric helps illustrate these problems. CWT is the period from the time the mechanic's supply clerk enters the requisition into the Unit-Level Logistics System (ULLS) or Standard Army Maintenance System (SAMS) computers until the materiel is processed and available to that clerk at his or her supply-support activity or FDA (a local supply warehouse). CWT includes BO delays and encompasses all supply sources.[11] Figure 2.5 places the CWT metric within the generalized process flow diagram shown in Figure 2.1.

The process begins at the left side of Figure 2.5 with an equipment-maintenance activity that identifies the need for a part. The supply clerk then enters a request, which flows to the FDP and SARSS for processing. If the part is available, it will be issued from the FDP's inventory, the authorized stockage list (ASL); in this case, the CWT "clock" stops at the point at which SARSS releases the materiel release order (MRO). If the part is not available at the direct supporting FDP, automated supply-management actions search for sources at other local FDPs before routing the requisition to the IM for that specific national stock number (NSN). The IM at the national inventory-control point (NICP) searches storage depots, repair programs, and vendors to eventually satisfy the customer's requisition. The length of the CWT depends, in part, on how long it takes for this process to be completed.[12]

---

[10] These charts compare only BO rates. The number of requisitions processed by each of these organizations varies dramatically.

[11] CWT was developed to track the total time from the time a mechanic asks for a part until he or she has it in hand to perform a maintenance task. However, the current Army data system does not record the time between the part's arrival at the SSA and the mechanic's receipt of the part. These limitations are not preventing the Army from making continuous improvements to its process activities.

[12] For more explanation of CWT, see *CWT and RWT Metrics Measure the Performance of the Army's Logistics Chain for Spare Parts*, 2003.

Figure 2.5
Process Flow Diagram for Army Field-Level Customer Requisitions

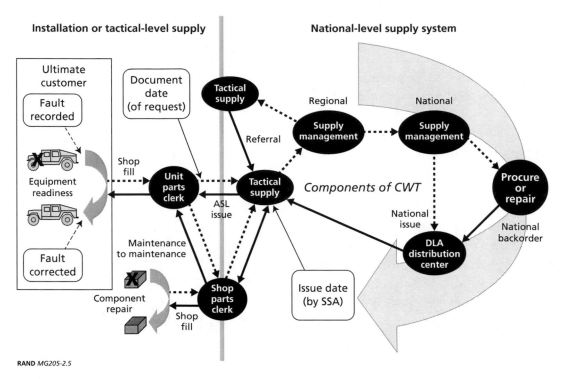

RAND *MG205-2.5*

Figure 2.6 illustrates the lengthy CWT that can be associated with a BO. The figure presents Class IX CWT performance between January and June 2002 in support of all customers at an installation with a mechanized infantry division.

The leftmost two bars show total overall CWT, sorted by AMC- and DLA-managed items. Each double set of bars following *Total CWT* displays CWT for each source of fill. The three-part bars show the variability in CWT. The top of each dark gray segment marks the point (in days) at which 50 percent of the requisitions were complete, while the top of each medium-gray segment marks the 75th percentile, and the top of each light-gray segment, the 95th percentile. The squares within the bars indicate mean performance, while the open ends above the bars indicate that the measurement extends beyond the 100-day scale presented. This chart also displays (as triangles) the percentage of requisitions filled from each source of fill. The percentages (right axis) for all of the sources sum to the 100 percent depicted in the *Total CWT* bars.

The 50th percentile for BOs extends past the 40-day mark, and the columns extend well beyond the 100-day scale of the figure for both DLA- and AMC-managed items requested by this division. The rightmost categories, DVD and Other, also

Figure 2.6
CWT Statistics for a Mechanized Infantry Division Installation

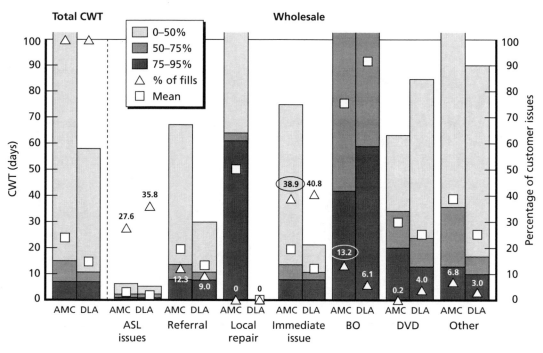

SOURCE: CTASC data, Ft. Stewart (January–June 2002).
RAND MG205-2.6

have some long CWTs. However, taken together, these categories comprise less than 10 percent of either the DLA- or Army-managed requisitions.[13]

For the period examined (January to June 2002), these customers received over 50 percent of their requisitions for AMC-managed items from wholesale sources, and approximately 25 percent of those wholesale-filled requisitions were BOs.[14] DLA performed better than AMC with respect to this CWT metric at this installation, with a BO rate of about 13 percent of national-level fills. This installation's CWT is basically consistent with the aggregate Army data shown in Figures 2.2 through 2.4, although the rates do vary from unit to unit because of equipment and other differences.[15]

---

[13] We do not know whether any of these were BOs. We only know the times involved, and because the numbers are small, they are not discussed further in this report.

[14] Wholesale immediate issues plus BOs, or 38.9 + 13.2 = 52.1, while 13.2/52.1 = 0.253 or ~25 percent.

[15] It is important to remember at this point that the BO rate shown in Figures 2.2 and 2.4 is calculated only with respect to the requisitions passed to wholesale; it does not include requisitions satisfied from local sources (i.e., ASL, referrals, and local repair).

Summary

The evidence presented in this chapter supports the anecdotal reports that retail Army customers have been facing higher-than-expected BO rates, particularly for reparable items. For at least some of these items, the number of repairs occurring at the depots is insufficient to meet demands. In other cases, the current reparable process has resulted in repairs in anticipation of customer needs that did not occur as projected, increasing (and wasting) inventory and repair investment. In the next chapter, we will examine the process used to set inventory levels and manage the depot-level reparable workload. This discussion will help to assess whether IMs are not planning sufficient quantity or whether other problems account for the insufficient supply of serviceable reparable items.

CHAPTER THREE

Understanding the Reparable-Management Process

To understand what is driving the Army's high BO rates, we need to examine the reparable-management process, which sets inventory levels and returns serviceable reparable assets to the shelf. This process brings the supply management and repair activities into a single integrated process. The intended output is the availability of adequate serviceable inventory to meet expected demands. This chapter defines the reparable-management process and identifies issues that impact its effective and efficient functioning.

In this analysis, we are attempting to respond explicitly to an evolving Army maintenance concept that calls for troubleshooting and parts replacement forward (in the field) and component repair to the rear (i.e., in support echelons that are removed physically from the engaged forward mission forces).[1] This concept is intended both to improve effectiveness by reducing the support footprint forward and to improve efficiency by consolidating repair capacity and capabilities. The shift to this new concept could ultimately produce changes in the reparable workload at the AMC depot level. Thus, the Army has specified the need for a highly responsive reparable process and repair activities that can quickly return items to a serviceable and ready-to-issue condition.[2]

---

[1] A maintenance concept and policies typically define some of the parameters that supporting repair processes should meet. Army Regulation 750-1, "Army Material Maintenance Policy" (dated August 18, 2003), was revised to incorporate this new view even as the concept continues to evolve. The previous policy in the July 1, 1996, version, Para 3-1h, was "Repair on site, whenever possible, using the lowest level maintenance activity that has the capability and authority to perform the work. *Repair forward* will minimize repair times by minimizing evacuation of materiel." The language contained in the new version, Para 3-1b, says the "emerging maintenance policy" will help reduce "the forward deployed logistics footprint. This emerging '*replace forward, repair rear*' policy will replace the Army's current 'fix forward' policy for future Army units." The same paragraph goes on to state "the Army is examining the elimination of our current four-level maintenance system in favor of a more-simplified two-level maintenance system" (emphasis added).

[2] This research does not explicitly address the issues of privatization or other alternatives to organic repair capacity or capability. It also does not address the projection of workload by location that might result from changing policy alternatives. In this study, we assumed that the current AMC installation alignment exists, and we attempted to determine what could be done within those conditions in the near term to bring about significant improvements in support performance. Further, we have attempted to find avenues for improvement within the context of existing information technology (IT) capabilities.

The Current Reparable-Management Process

The reparable-management process is ultimately driven by the need for reparables at tactical weapon-system or end-item repair activities, as illustrated in Figure 3.1.[3]

As shown in the left portion of the figure, evidence of an end-item fault or malfunction is discovered during equipment operation or within the larger context of maintenance-process activities (e.g., periodic inspections). The weapon system or end-item may be rendered completely inoperative or may be merely degraded in

Figure 3.1
Key Activities of the Current Reparable-Management Process

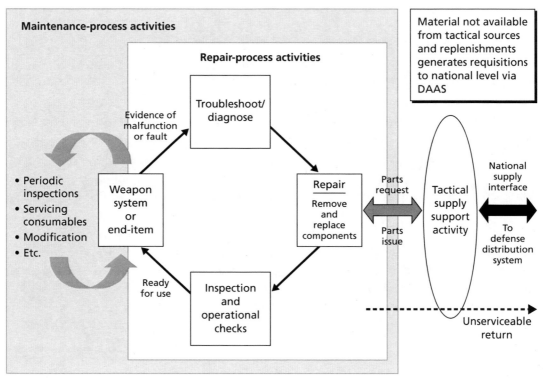

RAND *MG205-3.1*

---

[3] There are other sources of demand for reparable assets (e.g., end-item overhaul and modification programs and foreign military sales (FMSs)). However, Figure 3.1 shows the classic rationale for the reparable-management process as an approach for sustaining military operations.

capability. In either case, a repair action, shown in the middle portion of the figure, is required to return the item to its intended level of capability.[4]

In initiating a repair action, an individual with the necessary technical skills and equipment typically performs a three-step series of activities to (1) determine precisely what is wrong and what must be done to restore capabilities (including ordering necessary parts); (2) perform the actual repair tasks (which often involve the removal and replacement of parts or components); and (3) inspect and operationally check to ensure that the required capability has been restored.

Step 2 is of primary interest in this discussion. If a mechanic determines that a serviceable reparable is needed to complete the repair of an end-item, he or she will order the part. Ideally, the replacement part or component will be available in either tactical-level or national-level inventories of serviceable spares. This activity is illustrated on the right-hand side of Figure 3.1. Tactical-level inventories are replenished from the national level, and the national level is replenished by a separate set of repair activities.

Figure 3.2 provides a detailed view of the order-fulfillment process, including that for reparable assets, at the tactical level.[5] The purpose of the reparable-management process is to respond appropriately to customer demands by repairing unserviceable returns to keep serviceable national inventory at required levels.[6] As the order-fulfillment process activities occur, the inventory records for the requisitioned items are adjusted to reflect the use of inventory with respect to both total system inventory and the level at the location tasked to fill the order.

---

[4] We use the term *maintenance* to refer to all the actions performed on equipment to ensure operability and to restore degraded conditions. Maintenance includes formal and informal inspections for condition, including scheduled services. It also includes the servicing of any consumable commodities such as fuel, oil, and water, as well as troubleshooting of malfunctions and the removal and replacement of items necessary to restore degraded conditions. Finally, it includes modifications, remanufacturing, and overhauls intended to upgrade capabilities, extend service life, or otherwise improve the condition of components or end-items. *Repair* is one component of the larger maintenance process; it refers to *actions that restore a malfunctioning item to serviceable condition.* A *repair cycle* begins when a malfunction is identified and includes all actions necessary to return the item to serviceable condition. In the case of component repair, it also includes positioning of components for potential issue against a future requirement. In other words, the repair cycle involves all actions required throughout the full broken-to-fixed cycle for both end-items and components.

[5] Detailed discussion of the order-fulfillment process can be found in in Wang, 2000, and Dumond, Brauner, Eden, et al., 2001. This report focuses on the use of critical information generated within the order-fulfillment process to signal the reparable-management process that inventory replenishment action is required. This is an example of the interdependence among the various Army logistics-system processes.

[6] Inventories for resources other than reparable assets must also be restored via appropriate process activities. However, these activities are not illustrated or discussed here.

Figure 3.2
Reparable-Management Process Activities to Replenish Serviceable Inventories

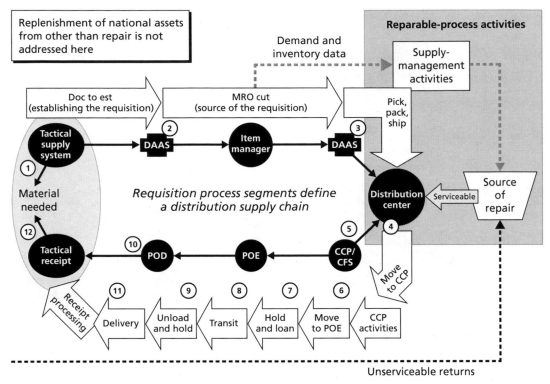

RAND *MG205-3.2*

Figure 3.3 provides a high-level view of the reparable-management process that focuses attention on its two critical components, supply-management activities and repair activities. The supply-management activities include both adjusting inventory requirements and initiating actions for item repairs and vendor procurements that meet those requirements. This view also emphasizes the other primary process input in the reparable-management process: the unserviceable return or malfunctioning component that is repaired and returned to inventory to meet future customer demands.

A mechanic's ability to complete an end-item repair can hinge on whether or not a reparable component is available and how long the mechanic will have to wait to receive it. Thus, the end-item repair process depends critically on having sufficient numbers of serviceable reparables, which depends, in turn, on the effectiveness and responsiveness of the process for planning and executing depot-level reparable workload. This process is discussed below.

Figure 3.3
Supply-Management and Repair Activities of the Reparable-Management Process

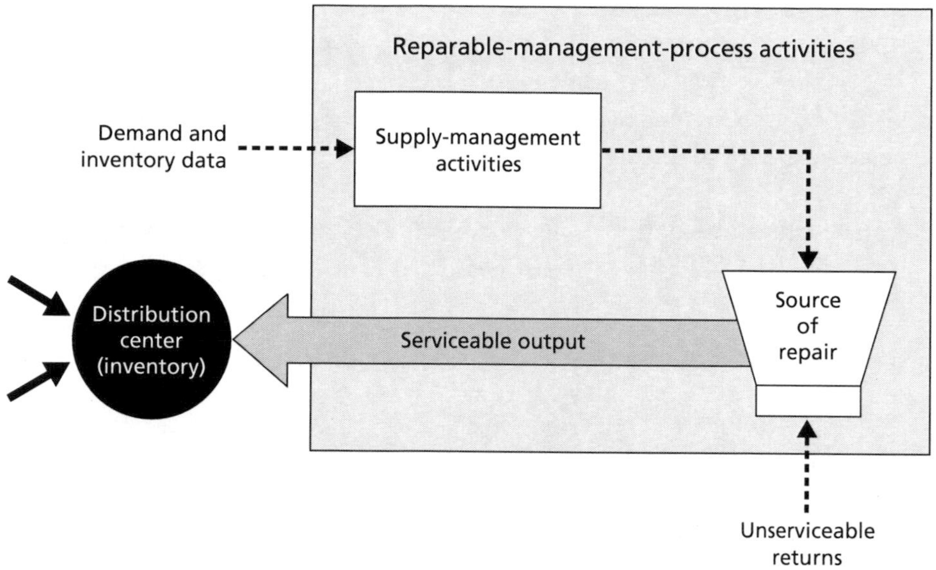

RAND *MG205-3.3*

Depot-Level Reparable Workload

The process for managing the depot-level reparable workload has two main components: planning and execution. The planning activities address a long time horizon, with a primary focus on long-term needs, such as budget and capacity issues, and some short-term issues, such as monthly replanning. Execution activities address the near-term issues that allow the process to be responsive to the uncertainty of actual customer demands and nonforecast mission needs. The execution activities also include the repair activities at the source of repair.

Planning for Both Near-Term and Long-Term Needs

The current planning process for a reparable is intended to address both near-term and long-term needs. It produces recommendations for inventory levels and repair and/or vendor buy quantities, and it also provides input to the Army working-capital fund (AWCF) budget process and to program-objective memorandum (POM) budget planning, which has a rolling six-year planning horizon. The POM feeds the Planning, Programming, and Budgeting System (PPBS) and eventually the congressional appropriations process. The reparable planning activity results in a formal decision package for approval of a repair program known as a procurement-request order number (PRON).[7] In addition, the reparable planning activity ultimately considers vendor replenishment needs for the reparable, adjustments to repair capacity, and other long-lead-time planning considerations. When a repair PRON has management approval, it is typically scheduled to begin execution 18 months later, at the beginning of the new fiscal year that was the focus of the planning scenario.

The responsible item manager (IM) initiates reparable workload planning for Army-managed items.[8] The planning sequence used by IMs at TACOM is shown in Figure 3.4.

IMs rely on several information tools during the planning process for a reparable. In initiating planning activities, IMs use the Commodity Command Standard

Figure 3.4
Tools Used by Item Managers to Understand Demand Patterns (Planning Sequence for Repair-Process Program Development by TACOM IM)

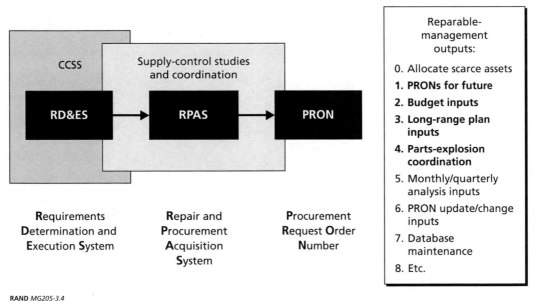

---

[7] A reparable PRON usually deals with a single reparable NIIN. However, some complex NIINs can include other reparable NIINs as components.

[8] The IM exercises broad responsibility for the management of relatively large numbers of individual Army-managed assets as part of a larger IM team. The IM maintains the data files for each item and monitors the day-to-day condition of inventories. As necessary, the IM performs supply-control studies that initiate and document relevant actions concerning inventory items (e.g., changes to inventory requirements, initiation of vendor replenishment, repair program changes). Experienced supervision is applied throughout the process, with supervisors reviewing the IM's efforts.

System (CCSS),[9] a mainframe-based software system that collects data on supply transactions and executes multiple batches of transactions throughout each workday. Periodically, IMs also use auxiliary programs, including the Requirements Determination and Execution System (RD&ES). RD&ES usually assesses all NSNs on a monthly basis, as scheduled by the IM.[10] Database maintenance performed prior to an RD&ES analysis is a critical and potentially very large task. Although data elements such as demands are updated automatically, many parts of the database maintenance must be completed manually. After each RD&ES analysis, the IM reviews the output to identify problems and necessary action.

The output from RD&ES includes recommendations for changes in inventory requirements and repair and/or vendor buy quantities.[11] The RD&ES output becomes the primary input to the manual supply-control study that is the basis of the decision package prepared by the IM for coordination and the eventual approval of an official repair program, or PRON. For repair recommendations, the output includes a monthly-recommended repair schedule for the remainder of the current fiscal year and the next full fiscal year.

At TACOM, a spreadsheet-type model called the Repair and Procurement Acquisition System (RPAS) (shown in the middle of Figure 3.4) is used to integrate RD&ES data into a rolling six-year budget plan appropriate for its inputs to the POM and the formal budget process. Running the RD&ES output through RPAS creates the workload levels necessary to project yearly amounts for a budget plan based on the most recent forecast of future demand.

The IM uses all available relevant data to build a formal decision package for the approval of a PRON, shown at the right of Figure 3.4. An approved PRON authorizes the execution of a repair-program quantity (i.e., approval is granted to a source of repair to expend resources for this purpose and for the IM to pay or reimburse for those expenditures upon delivery of serviceables). Final approval of the PRON occurs above the IM in the decision hierarchy of TACOM or the relevant MSC. The MSC and repair-depot representatives review the PRON recommenda-

---

[9] An initiative is under way to replace the CCSS with a more modern system. While the initial fielding of new capabilities began at CECOM during May 2003, neither the technical specification for the replacement system nor a firm implementation schedule is currently available. Therefore, this discussion addresses the current IT and procedures.

[10] In the past, consumable items were analyzed monthly, while reparables were analyzed quarterly; now AMC calls for monthly analysis of all AMC-managed items. In the context of the IM's total workload, there has been a perceived constraint on the time available for more-frequent item analysis. In addition, the analytic complexity of reparable items is now greater, and the quarterly cycle reduced CCSS costs. It is recognized (e.g., from the reparable BO rates) that more-frequent review is necessary to address customer needs.

[11] It is logically consistent for RD&ES to recommend repairs for a given NIIN and also to recognize that a vendor buy of additional assets is required to maintain the total stockage basis of serviceable assets. If the CCSS database is accurately maintained, RD&ES can provide information on the rate of condemnations during repair, return and repair pipeline times, changing demand rates, and other relevant information.

tions; approved PRONs are scheduled for implementation at the beginning of the new fiscal year 18 months later, consistent with the budget process.

A PRON can be viewed as an evolving decision document that can become a "license" to expend the resources necessary to repair assets and thereby return serviceables to the shelf for issue to customers repairing end-items at the Army tactical level and to others, such as other services and FMSs. The process of reviewing and approving PRONs requires a number of questions to be answered concerning funds, depot repair capacity, repair-parts availability, and the status of previous PRONs. The final approved program reflects changes resulting from constrained resources in the context of thousands of potential repair programs and replenishments through vendor procurements.

The annual long-range planning process for reparable items typically begins with the April run of RD&ES, at which point the demands and other historic data elements are current as of the end of March. Since the repair program planned beginning in April of a given year will not be released as an approved PRON until the start of the following fiscal year, the IM often has three PRONs going for a given NIIN at once: the current-fiscal-year program that is executing, the last completed planning effort that is expected to begin execution at the start of the next fiscal year, and the current planning effort that will become the PRON for the following fiscal year. The data should necessarily integrate across these PRON efforts. Likewise, the continuing coordination efforts must be simultaneously reconciled across the three time horizons. A particular IM is likely to be working this PRON process for dozens of NIINs at the same time.

The planning process for reparables also addresses some short-term issues. In addition to participating in the formal PRON development activities, the IM has the opportunity to develop and submit decision packages on a monthly basis to change the current or planned PRON for a reparable item. At TACOM, these packages are reviewed within the IM's organization and are prioritized for action. Critical needs could result in immediate staffing and coordination to replan aspects of the PRON to address customer needs. In general, the decision packages are prioritized, and the most important packages are addressed at monthly and quarterly reviews. Decisions to change quantity or repair schedule are made after coordination and approval by the supply, repair, and financial managers involved.

Execution of Repair Programs

Repairs cannot begin until the budget is approved by Congress, the authority AMC requires to execute its repair programs. Even though these AMC activities are funded via the AWCF, the congressional appropriation funds the necessary repair-parts procurement. Furthermore, the individual yearly PRONs are not typically released to the depots all at once. Although practice varies, the MSC will often initially release only the first six months of spending authority for a PRON. While appropriation-funded customers typically have congressional authority (from a continuing resolution) to continue mission activities and to requisition materiel to support those activities, the depot-level repair activity is not typically permitted to begin execution until the budget is passed, because of a restriction on the procurement of repair parts and a mix of DoD, Army, and local policies. Therefore, at the end of a fiscal year, repair-depot managers have an incentive to carry over some previously approved and funded workload to occupy the available workforce.[12]

Once the repair depot receives authorization to proceed, it usually begins the execution process by placing parts on order to support the new work and accelerating the completion of the previous, or "carryover," PRON work that managers have been stretching beyond the previous October to keep the workforce busy. The PRONs are typically scheduled to level the rate of production across the period. A centralized planning and scheduling staff at the repair depot handles overall depot capacity and issues across work centers. Within the various work centers, certain individuals are designated to handle the daily interface between the shop, the centralized planning and scheduling staff, and the supporting supply activities. The shop scheduler is the IM counterpart at the repair depot. This is the person who initiates contacts with DLA to have unserviceables delivered to the shop, ensures that repair parts are available, maintains records on condemnations or washouts, and works with DLA to deliver serviceables.

When the depot is ready to begin new work, the shop scheduler calls for a batch of unserviceables or reparable carcasses to be shipped from the DLA storage facility. There are generally two reasons for inducting in batches. The first relates directly to the need for repair parts. When the carcasses arrive from storage, each is disassembled, cleaned, and inspected to determine its specific repair needs. Each newly inducted carcass then becomes not only an item to be repaired, but also a potential donor of parts needed to repair other carcasses (a workaround activity known as a "rob back"). Second, DLA charges per batch or delivery for withdrawing carcasses from

---

[12] The financial authority for depot repairs is ultimately a complex issue. Fundamentally, "no one may obligate funds in excess of or in advance of an appropriation or in excess of an apportionment or a formal submission of funds," in accordance with the Antideficiency Act codified in Title 31 United States Code (USC) and implemented by Office of Management and Budget (OMB) Circular A-34, DoD Directive 7200.1, and Volume 14 of the DoD Financial Management Regulation (FMR) (DoD 7000.14-R).

The depot repair of Army reparables to support tactical customers is an AWCF activity, not an appropriated-fund activity. However, the depot workload is a complex mix of appropriated and WCF tasks. The demarcation of funding among tasks in the depot workload is not always clear and segregated. For example, an engine repaired and used in an M88A1 rebuild program is ultimately funded by appropriated funds, while the same type of engine (i.e., same NIIN) repaired to replenish serviceable inventory in support of future tactical customer demands is AWCF workload. Furthermore, the DoD FMR Volume 11B, Chapter 13 (par. 130102D) states, "DWCF depot maintenance or repair does not fund the procurement of parts."

If a continuing or other resolution permits customers to buy from AWCF inventories, it would seem that these revolving-fund activities should have mechanisms to replenish those same items in anticipation of continuing needs, whether the items are reparable or consumable. Military readiness is not well served by deferring repairs of parts that have due-outs to tactical customers.

storage and taking them to the repair shop. The pricing policy allows depot managers to save a little on repair expenses by minimizing the number of DLA transaction charges.

As unserviceables enter the repair process, they "explode" into an inventory of component parts and assemblies that constitute work-in-process (WIP) inventory whose location and condition must be managed if serviceable assets are to efficiently emerge from the process as intended. Many of the parts that constitute a reparable item are intended for reclamation or reuse in the course of the repair. An initial disassembly and inspection is required to determine exactly which reclaimable parts will be recovered and which will be condemned. Unserviceables may need to be inducted before all requisitioned consumable repair parts arrive, because the lead time to reclaim some parts is long and variable, and some parts will need to be replaced due to condemnation.

When the depot shop completes a repair, the repaired item is packaged to defined standards and returned to DLA for processing to serviceable-asset status. The IM is notified by DLA that serviceable assets are being added to the record. The IM then notifies DLA as to the disposition of the completed items. The IM might direct the immediate shipment of an item to satisfy a customer due-out (i.e., a BO), or the item might be moved to a distribution center at another location for future issue, or it might merely be left in storage at the DLA distribution center supporting the repair depot.

Figure 3.5 illustrates the flow of activities typical for depot-level repairs. The depot-level maintenance activity is very similar to that shown in Figure 3.1 for the tactical level. At both levels, the workload can involve weapon systems, end-items, or reparables. Unserviceable reparable components inducted for a PRON designed to produce serviceable inventory are returned to serviceable inventory after repair. During the course of end-item overhauls, these same components (i.e., NIINs) may need to be repaired and returned to an end-item. The funding for this type of repairs is included under the PRON for the end-item overhaul.

Summary

This chapter has presented a high-level view of the current processes for planning and execution of reparable management. The next two chapters address the supply-management processes used to support responsive depot repair and the repair activities. A case study is used to provide a consistent example across both chapters that illustrates how the current process has been functioning. Finally, some improvement alternatives suggested by commercial practice and the literature are identified.

Figure 3.5
Depot-Level Maintenance and Repair Activities

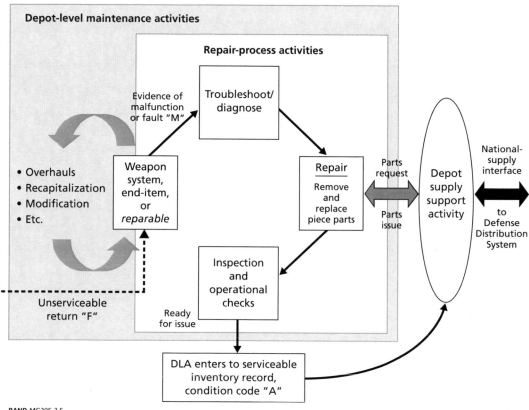

RAND *MG205-3.5*

CHAPTER FOUR

Improving Planning Activities

This chapter and Chapter Five show how the reparable-management process as a whole can become more responsive to requirements. Some of the alternatives for improvement we present emerged from interaction with managers and technicians within the system and some were identified from accounts of better-performing commercial entities.

To provide a deeper understanding of the reparable-management process, we use a case study of the M88A1 diesel engine. Our analysis of this case identified three critical issues in the reparable-management process:

- Inaccurate long-term planning forecasts due to the length of the planning horizon and uncertainty in customer demands.
- A lack of separation between planning and execution in supply-management activities.
- Insufficient repair responsiveness to meet customer needs.

We address the first two issues in this chapter and the third issue in Chapter Five.

Key Issues in the Current Process for Planning and Execution of PRONs to Repair Reparable Items

Uncertainty in Customer Demands on Long-Term Planning Forecasts

As shown in Figure 4.1, customer demand for the M88A1 diesel engine is highly uncertain. The vertical bars show the actual monthly requisitions seen by the IM. The average demand forecasts are derived from the RD&ES calculation and are based on exponential smoothing or an exponentially weighted moving average of recent demand history.[1] The planning process lead time for the FY2000 PRON is also indi-

---

[1] TACOM technicians identified the type of model used by CCSS for this purpose. The database also confirmed that the previous period's forecast, the current-period actual demand, and a smoothing factor were present. Actual code was not available for review.

Figure 4.1
Variability in Demand for the FY2000 Reparable M88A1

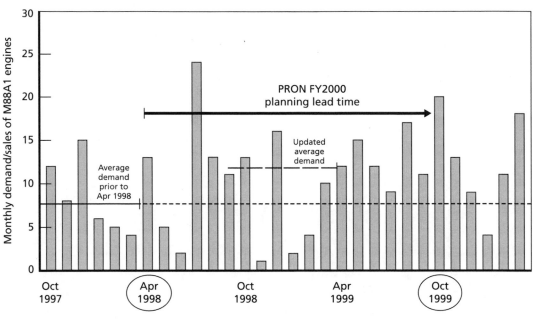

SOURCE: LIF, completed wholesale sales.
RAND *MG205-4.1*

cated. That process began in April 1998, with the target of implementation in October 1999 (i.e., the start of FY2000).

Uncertainty and variability in demand means that the forecast demand rate only occasionally matches the actual demand in any particular month. The average demand rate for M88A1 engines calculated in April 1998 was about eight per month, and the planning process assumed that this rate would continue into the foreseeable future. However, by the time the FY2000 PRON was being implemented, the customer demand rate had increased to about 12 engines per month (about a 50 percent increase).

In this case, the average demand increased, but reductions in demand can just as readily be found in the overall population of reparable NIINs. Demand for reparable

---

Most standard undergraduate or graduate-level texts on operations research or operations management provide comparative discussions of standard forecasting techniques. See, for example, Stevenson, 2002. An exponential-smoothing approach is quite reasonable for this application. However, the inherent variability in the data can still result in significant forecasting errors, especially for forecasts far into the future (e.g., beyond three to six months). Furthermore, this use of a single forecasting model is a compromise. If one is dealing with NIINs that exhibit seasonality or trends or other obvious known demand patterns, better-performing algorithms could be used for those NIINs with better results. However, CCSS uses a single forecasting model in its current form. Even with multiple models as options, both the variability and the other environmental factors associated with the military operating scenario result in uncertainty in demands over time.

items usually derives from malfunctions associated with events such as periodic inspections, training events, exercises, deployments, and various mission scenarios.

Although this case study addresses a single low-tech NIIN, the high variability and uncertainty (i.e., nonstationary mean) seen should not be considered atypical.[2] The quantity of most military equipment types is relatively small at the dispersed tactical-level units, and therefore demand statistics at that level can be misleading. Across the whole U.S. military establishment, the numbers of demands are usually large enough to build some confidence in expected or average demand, but variance is additive, and the observed variability then tends to be significant. Furthermore, changes in average demand, as seen in this case study, are not always logically explainable or known in advance, and this leads to significant uncertainty.

The point of this discussion is not about recognizing emerging trends but about recognizing the inevitable difficulty of precisely forecasting demand.[3] Army equipment usage is not relatively constant in rate or duration over time. In peacetime, equipment is used in training activities that tend to be infrequent and episodic. When equipment is deployed in combat operations, the pace of use can easily increase by a factor of ten or more. Furthermore, not all training or combat operations use all equipment components at the same rate. Therefore, merely knowing general operating statistics will not necessarily translate into uniformly better forecasts of malfunctions and reparable-part demands.

A smoothed production plan, such as that used in the current reparables process, tends not to cohere well with the uncertainty of demand. An example of the planning process is shown in Figure 4.2. As noted earlier, at certain times of the year, an IM has two repair planning packages in progress at the same time, one that was just initiated in April of the current year and one initiated in April of the previous year and now approaching the final formal decision stage and the start of implementation. In addition, as a result of an earlier planning cycle, the IM is also dealing with an active PRON that is being executed.

The solid horizontal bars labeled *Average demand* in Figure 4.2 indicate the average customer demands available to the RD&ES model calculation at the start of each planning cycle, and the dotted lines that begin where the average-demand lines end each April represent the forecasts the model predicted based upon those demands. In this case, from April 1998 to April 1999, the average demand for these engines increased by more than 25 percent. By mid-FY2000, the average demand had grown from eight engines per month to more than 18 per month.

---

[2] Crawford, 1988.

[3] We are not suggesting that more-relevant data and more-sophisticated modeling could not provide significantly better statistics and predictive capability.

Figure 4.2
The Repair-Planning Processes for Different PRONs

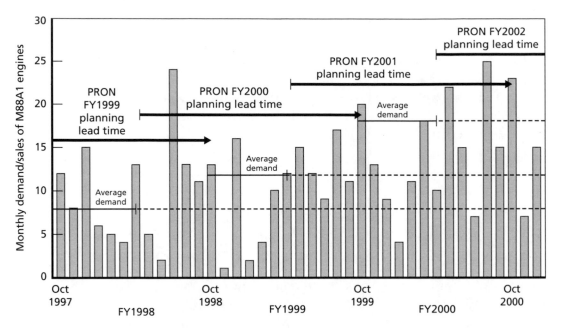

SOURCE: Notional data based on LIF, completed sales.
RAND *MG205-4.2*

The net result of this situation is seen in Figure 4.3. The approved monthly-level PRON production program for FY2000 is shown, along with the actual due-outs (i.e., customer BOs) plus the cumulative monthly demands minus achieved production as recorded in CCSS. The program coordination and negotiation resulted in a FY2000 PRON to produce equal monthly quantities, a smoothed production plan that was characteristic of the majority of data reviewed. But the smoothed plan did not match well with actual demands.

The mismatch between the forecasts and actual demands grew worse over time. Note that the y-intercept of the actual demand plus BO is at 50 engines, which represents the fact that by October 1999, the IM had accumulated 38 due-outs or BOs to customers. In addition, the increasing customer demands during the year increasingly diverge from the PRON. The projected-demand line represents the projected sales from the April 2000 RD&ES output. The continued expected linear divergence indicated is based on the higher average sales and the fact that the number of engines repaired had not increased; changes to the FY2000 PRON had not occurred.

The RD&ES detailed forecasting capability (like that of any forecasting algorithm) is unreliable beyond a few months, and forecasts beyond 18 months are of

Figure 4.3
FY2000 M88A1 PRON vs. Actual Demands

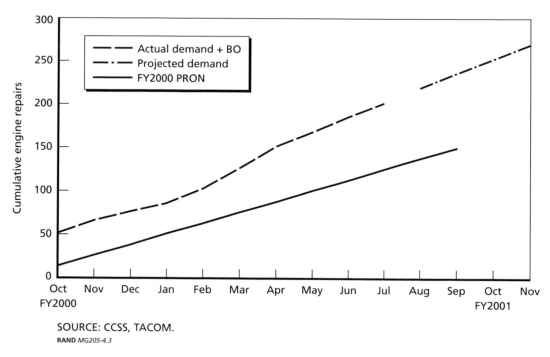

SOURCE: CCSS, TACOM.
RAND *MG205-4.3*

little practical use for detailed management decisions. This is not necessarily an indication that the wrong forecasting model is being used, however. We do not attempt in this study to recommend an optimal forecasting model or algorithm. Based upon the limited data we have seen, the current algorithm is reasonable, given the data and systems available.

The point is that no algorithm can yield a value that can be predicted as far in advance as Army procedures are trying to project without procedures for updating forecasts. Both variability in demand and the dynamic military operating environment argue against long-term forecast accuracy at the NIIN-level. While improvements may be possible and should be pursued at a moderate level of effort, the only available fix is to do more-frequent replanning. In forecasting and planning for the future, the Army should explicitly incorporate periodic replanning that allows the evolving plan to be informed by changes that would otherwise result in unfulfilled customer needs or overinvestment.

Although the forecasting component of the RD&ES module could probably be improved, the module is reasonable, and it provides useful monthly repair-quantity projections for the near term insofar as historical demands are useful in predicting future demands. Again, the change we recommend is to replan more frequently, in effect reducing the forecast horizon used for execution. RD&ES has the capability to take into account program changes in equipment density and intensity of operations, as well as other "planned" factors that would not otherwise be reflected in historical data when forecasting demand. The model also has explicit visibility of returned unserviceable assets available for induction into repair and historical recovery factors for projections.[4] The repair plans it provides are reasonably constrained by the availability of items to be repaired.

RD&ES does more than merely forecast demand; it also builds a repair plan to meet computed inventory requirements necessary to satisfy that demand. It looks at production capacity and repair times to determine whether simultaneous repair and vendor procurement is warranted to meet calculated expected demands.[5] RD&ES is also a reasonably effective tool for budget planning and aggregate planning tasks such as capacity planning—as long as all known factors are updated in the CCSS database.

At the present time, however, the model's forecasting abilities are limited because of insufficient data. Its basic sales forecast uses exponential smoothing to respond relatively quickly to changing demand patterns. Until recently, when the Single Stock Fund (SSF) initiative was fully implemented, the only sales figures available to the model (including due-outs) were at the national level.[6] Thus the model did not consider the true tactical customer demand rates, nor did it consider any assets repaired at an echelon below depot level. As a result, demands unknown to the IM could become a future production concern. For example, certain repairs made at the local level could be discontinued because of perceived quality deficiencies, and this would result in an increased demand rate at the depot level.

Need for Improved Supply-Management Planning and Execution

While the inadequacy of the long-term forecasts for production execution poses a problem in itself, there is also a need to place increased emphasis on near-term replanning, so that limited resources can be applied to respond to changing requirements as they emerge during the execution of the current PRON. Near-term replan-

---

[4] Unserviceable-asset returns currently occur only when the repairable assets come under the control of the IM, usually at a DLA distribution center, or when the IM directs a shipment from a forward location.

[5] This is a common condition for items with relatively high condemnation or washout rates during repairs (e.g., automotive generators/alternators, starters, etc.).

[6] SSF is an Army initiative that shifted the point of sale for the AWCF from national distribution centers closer to the customer. AMC now "owns" the inventory down to and including the ASL. Before SSF, AMC owned only the stocks in the DLA distribution centers, and consequently it saw only the sales from those locations in its transactional systems. These national wholesale sales do not equate to the total tactical sales, the total tactical demand, or the failure rate for a particular NSN. Therefore, IMs had a very limited view of the world upon which to base long-range plans.

The benefits of stock funding are discussed in Brauner, Pint, et al., 2000. Financial policy changes that could further improve the reparable-management process are discussed in Chapter Five.

ning can allow more-current information to be used in the replanning or execution decisions to adjust earlier plans to accord with the emerging reality at the NIIN level.

The current process tends to focus on budget planning; it is less responsive to changing customer needs that emerge during plan execution. During execution of a PRON, representatives from the MSC and the depot meet quarterly to revise schedules and address problem areas. These meetings include representatives of all the functional organizations needed to coordinate changes to the approved programs; thus, they would typically have been the venue, for example, at which to approve the rescheduled production necessary to get the M88A1 engine out of the persistent BO situation that developed. However, because IMs do not usually attend these meetings, issues about increasing production are discussed only if decision packages have been developed and coordinated. Unfortunately, only the most critical issues typically make the agenda, leaving many issues ignored until they have become critical problems and have garnered the attention of senior Army personnel. In the case of the M88A1 engine, the need to increase production did not surface soon enough.

Even though this NIIN had been averaging 30 or more due-outs per month for more than a year, the FY2000 PRON had been approved as planned, with no increase programmed to overcome the deficit associated with the increased demand. Thus it started in the hole. When we began our case study and walked through the details of the reparable-item repair process, this issue quickly emerged.

Alternatives to the current process do exist. On the basis of the IM's standard analysis, but with the added perspective provided by the process walk-through, the IM team initiated a change to the PRON quantity sufficient to cover all existing due-outs for the M88A1 engine. They walked this reprogramming action through the necessary coordination in less than a week in January 2000, and funds were available for immediate implementation.

The revised FY2000 PRON authorized increased monthly production sufficient to catch up with known customer due-outs and the current average demand rate by the end of the fiscal year. Figure 4.4 shows the revised PRON quantities. Anniston Army Depot (ANAD) was to increase production to accomplish the PRON by the end of September 2000 and get the repair program for the engine able to meet known customer demands.

However, once changes to the monthly production schedule were authorized, the concern became whether ANAD could produce sufficient additional engines to meet that schedule. A detailed discussion of the repair activities is addressed in Chapter Five. Here, we remain focused on the planning activities.

Figure 4.4
The FY2000 M88A1 Engine PRON Revised to Meet Customer Demands

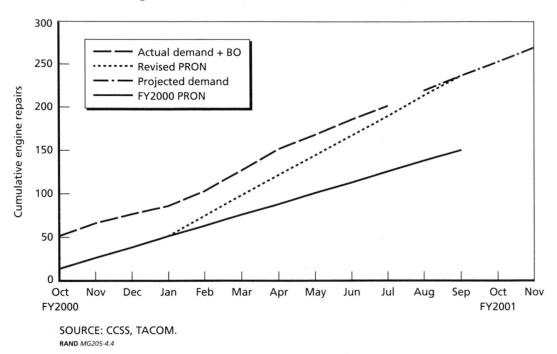

SOURCE: CCSS, TACOM.
RAND *MG205-4.4*

Approaches for Improving Supply-Management Planning and Execution

The problems associated with supporting customers with adequate serviceable reparable assets involve uncertainty and variability in both demand and supply of required items, as illustrated in Figure 4.1. In the future, engineers and logisticians might be able to reduce such levels of demand uncertainty, but no clear strategy currently exists to address this issue for any meaningful segment of the reparable inventory. Therefore, managers need to think about ways to improve forecasts or to improve responsiveness.

There is also uncertainty and variability in the supply of Army-managed items, particularly reparables. The BO rates demonstrated a pervasive pattern overall, and the M88A1 diesel-engine example illustrates the inability of the current management process to respond successfully to changes in demand with sufficient repair authorizations.

Furthermore, it is important to note that while this case study involved a NIIN that was experiencing a pattern of increasing demand, the reverse situation (where demand is significantly less than predicted) could be just as likely to occur. If repairs were executed against those overpredictions, production would exceed requirements. Neither excess nor insufficient production of serviceables is a desired condition. The desired outcome is that of efficiently meeting all requirements.

Although practical financial constraints always exist, funding has not emerged as one of the key issues in the process activities. However, that does not assure that the implementation of improvements will not require specific investments or reallocations of funds. It also does not mean that financial constraints could not be a key issue in the future and have not been at other times.

Successful commercial practice usually begins with performance-improvement efforts for similar problems that first address the uncertainty and responsiveness of supply (because the ability to assure supply to meet demands will usually improve a company's market share and profitability). As we look for ways to improve support to Army customers needing reparables, we follow a similar logic that seeks strategies to improve the AMC approach to uncertainty in supply, efficient strategies that will not result in net cost increases for the Army. We also identify some improvement alternatives suggested by commercial practice and the literature.

This study emphasizes actions that can be done immediately with minimal or no information technology (IT) changes. Our intent is to not permit the current lack of potential future "enablers" to prevent feasible improvement actions today.[7]

Approaches for Dealing with Uncertain Demand

Uncertainty and variability in customer demand affect most industries, and a number of alternatives have been developed and successfully used to address the problem. We discuss four basic approaches:

- Making forecasting models responsive to change.
- Adjusting safety stock.
- Reducing lead time and variability.
- Adjusting expectations.[8]

---

[7] The GAO has been encouraging process changes rather than merely IT change for many years. See, for example, GAO, 1993. RAND has provided the same message through the VM program. Published commercial examples over the past 15 years have become too numerous to list. Recommended sources include Womack et al., 1991; Womack and Jones, 1996; Kearns and Nadler, 1992; Keen, 1997; Byrne and Markham, 1991; and Pyzdek, 1999.

[8] Lists of strategies for coping with variability in operations are widely available. For an example of a consultant's view, see Dougherty, 2001, pp. 6–7. Academic texts in operations management offer similar taxonomies. Military tradition and writings provide similar coping strategies to handle the "fog of war" and other manifestations of variability that might impede mission accomplishment.

Frequent Updating of PRON Forecasts to Respond to Changing Demands

In the course of this research, we were told several times that the root cause of the problems of inadequate serviceable-reparable inventory is a bad forecasting model. This implies that the forecasting errors present in April 1998 are the underlying cause of the problems with FY2000 PRON execution. However, we know of no single forecasting algorithm that would provide sufficient accuracy to be useful over such an extended horizon for item-level predictions. Only knowing a causal factor ahead of time could improve the forecast.

In this application, AMC has traditionally used an exponential-smoothing model with historical demand data as the basis for projections about the future. In general, exponential smoothing is characterized by rapid response to changes in historic demand patterns (dependent on the choice of exponential coefficient and the weight given to more-recent demands). However, other models can provide better results, depending on the characteristics and assumptions about demand patterns.[9] For example, some models are designed to provide better predictive results for items with underlying seasonal or cyclic patterns (e.g., anti-freeze, sunscreen). Commercial software is available that uses multiple modeling options for each item, tracks the predictive accuracy over time, and dynamically chooses the currently best-performing option for making the next recommended forecast. In addition, experts are available to tailor new and unique models that will improve prediction accuracy.[10]

The literature suggests that the fundamental problem in this case is not the type of model used but the length of the planning horizon. As discussed in Chapter Three, using the current forecasting model to project inflexible repair schedules many months (and even years) into the future is not a reasonable approach. The long-range planning task needs a basis upon which to plan, not the basis necessary for perfect projections of the future. In the commercial world, budgets are often replanned to respond to emerging "truth" about the future; budgets can thereby be adjusted to the same reality that is facing sales and production in the near term. In the commercial world, even the long-lead-time investment decisions are revisited for modification as reality proves that forecast errors exist.

While the current forecasting model was seen to prove inadequate in the case of the M88A1 engine, it does not seem to be a wholly unreasonable tool for long-range aggregate budget planning that builds the POM and budget input. One would expect that at the aggregate level, some of the item forecasting errors would actually

---

[9] For example see Delurgio, 1998; Georgoff and Murdick, 1986, pp. 110–120; and Makridakis and Wheelwright, 1978.

[10] The discussion here has focused primarily on the choice of forecasting algorithm. The literature and commercial practice reflect increased interest in collaborative forecasting. The recommendations discussed below incorporate the basic concepts of collaborative forecasting and thereby imply changes to current forecasting policy. For further discussion see Mentzer and Bienstock, 1998.

cancel each other out, and the resulting aggregate or "bundle" of item PRONs could be a reasonable budget estimate.[11] However, the individual PRONs would still be expected to have high levels of forecasting error. Thus, the basic problem with the forecasting model appears to be not its capabilities for long-range planning and governmental budget development, but its usefulness in the execution of individual PRONs without near-term replanning.[12] The preferred approach seems to be to change procedures to use the best available prediction for the purpose at hand, rather than seeking a replacement model.

As noted above, the RD&ES model currently in use has the capability to include frequent updates, and the near-term predictions reviewed during our case study demonstrated responsive output. The RD&ES algorithm implementation can respond to changing demands and has built-in mechanisms to supplement the historical demand prediction with known changes in requirements (e.g., planned changes in operating tempo or scenarios that are expected to change future demand patterns, or changes to the level of fielded-unit equipment sets). What is needed is a more dynamic reparable-management process that attempts to meet emerging demands with decision rules and policies that constrain responsiveness only insofar as appropriations and the governing public law require.

Improving Service Level by Increasing Safety Stock

Variability in demand can also be addressed through safety stock, i.e., inventory that is held to buffer a process activity from uncertainty. As shown in Figure 3.2, the process activity of concern to us is the availability of serviceable spares at the national-level distribution centers where customer requisitions or tactical-level replenishments can be sourced. If no inventory is carried at this level, each requisition depends on a very accurate prediction of the next demand occurrence or a very responsive repair system. The RD&ES module has the capability to call for inclusion of safety-stock needs within the planning calculation. However, we found that the reparable items reviewed in our case study had no safety-stock level (i.e., the safety-stock requirement for those items was zero).[13] In addition, it should be noted that current repair batch size for replenishment of serviceable inventory does in itself pro-

---

[11] We did not pursue this hypothesis, because our emphasis was on finding opportunities for improvement within the context of the existing system structure. Hence the focus of this report is on near-term management issues.

[12] From an aggregate perspective, though, the forecasting model will still have significant problems when underlying causal factors (e.g., a change in operating tempo) change, and thus the long-term trend changes.

[13] That does not mean that there was no serviceable inventory available for all NIINs for which the safety-stock variable was zero. Due to the variability issues discussed above, the majority of items did not have zero on-hand inventory when the next requisition was received. Raising the safety stock above zero for a larger percentage of NIINs reduces the probability of a BO in the future, all other factors being equal. This is achieved by increasing the depth of inventory and inventory investment.

vide a level of safety stock inherent in its calculation. The multiechelon inventory structure, with reparable assets positioned forward at the tactical level, also provides an inventory buffer.[14]

Improving Replenishment Lead Times

The Army's reparable-management process could also be a very good candidate for a process-improvement effort focused on lead-time reduction. Lead-time-reduction approaches look at the chain of events necessary to meet a need and try to determine where it is most efficient and effective to insert buffers or reduce constraints so that the desired response time is met at lower total cost.[15] Lead-time reduction helps to minimize the early commitment of assets and facilitates the adjustment of production schedules until actual customer demands are received.

Such approaches typically involve frequent replanning inside the budget planning process and seek to gain closer feedback, where possible, on realized customer demands. Many commercial-sector organizations have applied these techniques to a wide range of activities, from retail sales (e.g., Wal-Mart and most major grocery chains use of point-of-sale data at their own distribution centers and provide this information directly to their vendor partners) to manufacturing (e.g., Toyota, Dell Computers), from entertainment (e.g., Blockbuster video rentals, cable TV on-demand programming) to remanufacturing of reparables (e.g., Cummins Diesel, Gateway computers, General Electric X-ray equipment), and many more.

It can be difficult to define and develop new decision strategies and to identify appropriate means of implementing the desired changes. Many of the most effective changes seem to occur across functional and/or organizational boundaries. In this case, the identification of ways to improve supply responsiveness for reparable items involve both supply and repair management issues. Thus, one challenge lies in the management team's ability to conceive of radically different solutions instead of incremental improvements or cost-reduction efforts within their limited organizational context. Unfortunately, many such cost-reduction schemes result in local-activity efficiencies rather than system savings, or the cost accounting system confuses the decision process with inappropriate data concerning alternatives.[16]

---

[14] For a further discussion of multiechelon inventory analysis see, for example, Sherbrooke, 1992; and Hillier and Lieberman, 2001.

[15] *Lead time* is specifically defined as the time between ordering a good or service and receiving it. Increasing finished-goods inventory (e.g., by holding safety stock) is a common example of using a buffer in the manufacturing and distribution processes to reduce lead time. However, such inventory has a cost, and operations managers are always in search of alternative ways to provide the required outputs at reduced costs. The discussion in this section is only illustrative of such alternatives. A number of operations-management texts are available, e.g., Stevenson, 2002.

[16] The literature includes sources of ideas for alternative strategies, as do professional organizations (e.g., the Council of Logistics Management (CLM), the American Production and Inventory Control Society (APICS)) and consultants. Nonetheless, it can be difficult to find an acceptable strategy, especially one that can be imple-

Applying a new approach to the reparable-management process would require taking a very close look at all the process activities needed to return an asset that has been determined to be unserviceable and complete all actions necessary to return it to a DLA distribution center in serviceable condition and ready for future issue. In our case study, the M88A1 engine had unserviceable assets available in storage at the DLA warehouse at the Army repair depot. The first action to indicate lead-time reduction in this instance was recognition among the management team that a persistent condition existed (i.e., multiple customer BOs awaiting repairs and the failure to authorize sufficient repairs to meet known demands).

Information about the size and nature of the BO problem was available through CCSS reports and IM-generated supply-control studies. However, the problem was not addressed because of the total volume of such information (which involved many different NIINs), financial constraints, and a focus on improving the long-term planning process (i.e., improving the forecasting model). Lead time could be reduced by developing ways to use the available information in more proactive ways to provide just the required serviceable-inventory levels, neither too high nor too low. Routine mechanisms are necessary that encourage replanning and repair coordination between the management-team members at the inventory-planning and repair-scheduling activities rather than extensive coordination and management approval mechanisms.[17]

Improving Communication About Customer Needs and Requirements

Although in some industries it is possible to influence customer demand patterns through advertising, pricing, or other means, such strategies are in most respects not available to Army materiel managers. The Army operations being supported are characterized by highly variable and uncertain customer demand patterns for reparables—and for military materiel in general. Although some items tend to experience more variability and uncertainty in demand than others, and while some items with highly uncertain demand may lend themselves to different forecasting techniques or combinations of coping strategies to mitigate the impact, generally speaking, the management team must expect variations associated with forecast error.

In light of such realities, one important mitigation strategy is to adjust expectations about what the forecasting model *should* be able to do and to gain better infor-

---

mented across organizational boundaries. One possible strategy, lean manufacturing, is discussed in greater detail in Chapter Five.

[17] The example discussed here (in the context of supply-management planning) relates to reduction of the planning and replanning lead time. However, all activities in the process that increase the total lead time required to replenish serviceable assets are fair game for improvement initiatives. Without reduction in lead time, supply managers will need to embrace other options to achieve comparable improvements in customer service. This illustrates the interaction of supply and repair management efforts necessary for reparable-management-process improvement.

mation about current and expected requirements. Acknowledgment of the limitations on accurately predicting the future can be the motivation necessary for a management team to collaborate in process-improvement efforts. Success in such efforts often hinges on finding ways to better use the information that becomes available to replan and adjust to be more responsive to the customers.

Both long- and near-term planning activities can benefit from improved information. Therefore, these activities must have the most-recent requirements and forecast information, even though it may impact them in different ways. Even after a long-range budget-planning milestone has past, significant changes to the forecast may provide critical information about the need to develop alternatives for reprogramming funds or other strategies. Updated information is of critical importance in the near-term replanning necessary to meet requirements as efficiently as possible.

Moving from Planning to Execution

The dominant issue facing the current reparable-management process is the contrast between the detailed, long-range planning activities that result in the approved PRON and the very different reality of the sales that generate the actual (and variable) demand for repairs. The efficient execution of the reparable-management plan requires repeated planning cycles with the most current information available. The system of planning tools should provide updated recommendations based on the near-term reality rather than on earlier long-range forecasts.

Figure 4.5 shows the reparable-management activities explained above and illustrated in Figures 3.3 and 3.4. A list of some key outputs is provided to illustrate the mix of near- and long-term issues that are being addressed. Outputs 1 through 4 are longer-range items. The other outputs are more directly related to the near-term issues involved in ensuring responsiveness to customers' changing needs. The ability to sort such outputs suggests a possible basis upon which to restructure the activities.

Linking Long-Term Planning to Near-Term Execution

One approach that holds promise for improving responsiveness is to recognize the links between long-term planning activities and near-term execution-process activities within the management structure. A disciplined planning process and a responsive execution process need not be mutually exclusive or physically separated. The execution process could continue within the constraints defined by the planning process (i.e., there is usually enough initial flexibility in the timing of production quantities within the approved PRON). However, when the planning-process results are shown to be incorrect in light of emerging information about customer demand, it should be possible to responsively adjust those plans.

**Figure 4.5
Current Reparable-Management Activities**

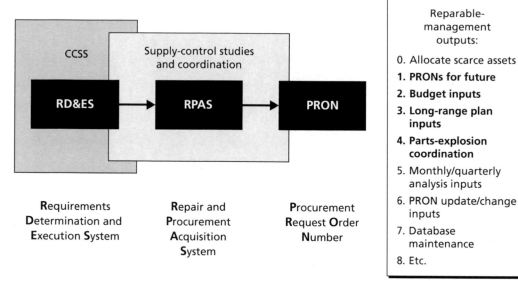

RAND *MG205-4.5*

Figure 4.6 depicts an alternative future environment in which production execution and scheduling have been separated from the long-range planning activities. The long-range planning process is shown at the top of the figure and is essentially the same as that currently in use. The execution process, on the bottom, takes a different form, one that accounts for the fact that execution activities are continuous and ongoing throughout the year. These activities are driven by daily demand data that flow continuously into CCSS (and the simultaneous obligation of customer funds that occurs when a requisition is submitted). Whereas the current process primarily uses quarterly meetings to approve production-schedule changes, the new view calls for deliberate movement toward more-frequent opportunities to reschedule. The use of the available feedback from RD&ES and CCSS will improve the responsiveness of the production process.

As Figure 4.6 implies, the Army should transition as quickly as possible to monthly schedule changes, using the available monthly RD&ES outputs that are now available. The availability of monthly RD&ES outputs does not automatically mean that procedures are in place to promptly process and implement those outputs. But one could envision a future management decision process that was informed weekly or even daily about customer demand and in which changes could be implemented when warranted. A daily process would reflect a true demand pull system. The quarterly meetings could then focus more on review and emerging constraints, enabling the IM team and the repair manager to be much more responsive to demand.

Figure 4.6
A More-Responsive Reparable-Management Process

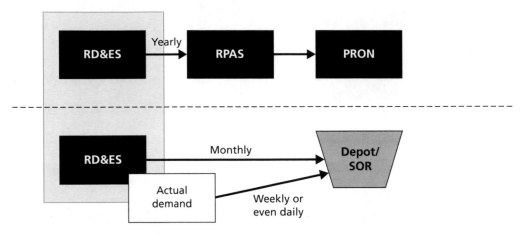

RAND MG205-4.6

Conclusion

This chapter has discussed the inventory-management activities dealing with both near-term and long-term planning. The critical message related to overall process improvement is that frequent replanning is needed to allow the most accurate information to inform the decisionmaking necessary to provide sufficient serviceable assets to meet customer demands. Also, a strategy is needed to promptly approve and execute the decisions that the frequent replanning enables. The alternatives explored in this chapter begin to point toward a reparable-management process that is more responsive to customer needs. Those needs may be either increasing or decreasing over the planning and execution time horizons. However, it should be clear from the discussion that improvement will require changes not only in the planning process but also in the repair process. We address the repair-process issue explicitly in the next chapter.

CHAPTER FIVE

Improving Repair Activities

In Chapter Four, we looked at the reparable-planning process in both the near and the long term. In this chapter, we focus on the issue of repair responsiveness. We again suggest some alternatives for improvement that emerged from interaction with the managers and technicians within the system and from the lessons of better-performing commercial entities.

Improving Repair-Activity Responsiveness to Deal with Uncertain Demand

Upon recognizing the increase in demand for the M88A1 diesel engine, the IM team responded by coordinating and implementing a change to the PRON that was being executed at the time. The intent was to authorize an increased repair quantity sufficient to meet the revised forecast demand by the end of the fiscal year (i.e., by the end of September 2000). After the PRON adjustment was implemented, the responsiveness of the reparable process became dependent upon the responsiveness of the repair activities.

During our process walk-through at ANAD, the local management team claimed to have sufficient facilities and manpower to meet the revised schedule. They had recently resolved a parts crisis that put them behind the original FY2000 PRON schedule and felt they were on track with all the assets they would need. However, we discovered that their procedures for inventory management and control were not sufficient to provide the visibility necessary to identify supply problems before they became critical to the production process. These procedures will be discussed in more detail below. For now, Figure 5.1 shows the repairs achieved for our M88A1 engine-repair case study under the original PRON and the revised PRON (from Figure 4.4) and adds a curve for achieved production through July 2000. Note that achieved production lagged behind the levels of both the FY2000 PRON and the revised PRON. In the following, we consider five interrelated approaches to making repair activities more responsive to customers' needs.

Figure 5.1
Repair Production at ANAD Under the FY2000 PRON and the Revised PRON

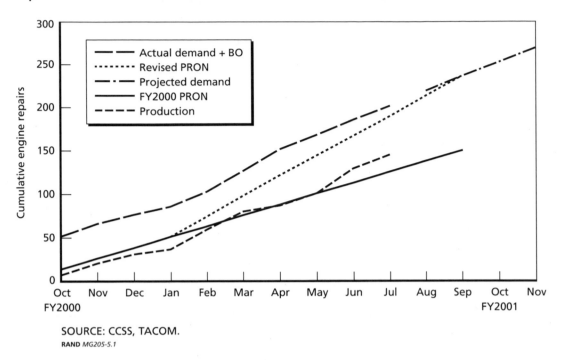

SOURCE: CCSS, TACOM.
RAND *MG205-5.1*

Approaches for Improving Repair-Activity Responsiveness

Several established alternatives have been successfully used to make repair activities more responsive to changing customer needs. Five of these are obvious candidates for application to the problem at hand:

- Reduce lead time for the next repair and reduce overall repair flow time.
- Use frequent replanning to keep production schedules and repairs synchronized with demand.
- Ensure the availability of unserviceable assets to support reparable activities.
- Improve the process for managing depot-level repair parts to support more-responsive repairs.
- Improve financial policies to support more-responsive depot repairs.

In addition to these possibilities, the discussion includes AMC's recently launched initiative to apply the principles of lean production and lean thinking to Army maintenance-depot operations. The AMC Commanding General (CG) directed the start of the Lean Line program on March 25, 2002. Fundamentally, *lean* applies to the value being created for the ultimate customer of a good or service. The lean approach considers all the actions taken to create that good or service in order to identify the activities that actually add value as defined by the customer. Any activity that absorbs resources but adds no value to the good or service is defined as waste or *muda*.[1] The objective of the lean approach is to reduce waste in order to increase production efficiency and shorten lead times. Batches of material are not pushed into the process, which would result in resources waiting to be processed; under the lean approach, induction is pulled, WIP is reduced, and all activities that do not add value are identified for future elimination.[2]

The AMC lean efforts provide an added dimension to the discussion of alternatives for improving the repair process. The tactical-level units—the ultimate customers for reparable assets—want and need to order reparable parts and have them issued promptly for use in restoring the operational capability of their mission equipment. The value to the customer is in timely availability, reliable condition and functionality, and an acceptable cost (not necessarily the lowest cost).

Reducing Lead Time for Next-Repair Completion and Overall Repair Flow Time

Applying flow-time reduction to the repair activities of the reparable-management process would involve first taking a very close look at all the process activities required to return a broken asset to serviceable status and turn it over to the DLA distribution center packaged and ready for issue. The goal should be to establish a mechanism that responds to customer needs by increasing production when demand increases, thus reducing the potential for BOs, and decreasing production when demand is not as great, thus minimizing excessive inventory investment.

The overall repair flow time includes the time from the induction of an unserviceable item into repair until it is ready to be placed back on the shelf at a distribution center as a serviceable item. If this total flow time is used for scheduling production to meet the next demand, availability of the next item is the full repair time away. In the case of the M88A1 diesel engine, this time would have been measured in weeks, mostly due to lengthy queuing or waiting times. However, the total time required to complete the sequence of actions needed to repair the next unserviceable M88A1 diesel engine is actually less than a day and is often between eight and 18 hours of work time. Thus, if the lengthy queuing or waiting times could be eliminated, the total repair lead time would be greatly reduced.

To reduce the time between repair activities, it is necessary to consider the sequence in which the repair activities take place. For example, the final testing activity for the M88A1 engine is running the completely assembled engine to check for basic operation, leaks, and power production. At this time, minor defects are fixed, adjustments are made, and the finished engine is containerized along with the appro-

---

[1] The lean literature frequently uses Japanese terms, because many of these practical concepts originated in Japan.

[2] "Lean thinking is *lean* because it provides a way to do more and more with less and less . . . while coming closer and closer to providing customers with exactly what they want" (Womack and Jones, 1996, p. 15).

priate documentation. DLA is then notified that the containerized engine is ready to be picked up and processed onto the inventory records as serviceable. If the activity immediately preceding the testing (i.e., the assembly activity) were to keep an engine finished and ready to move to the final testing, the lead time for the next asset would be on average one shift away instead of weeks away. Therefore, the lead time for the next asset repair would be much less than the total repair flow time for that asset.

For approved PRONs to repair multiple assets, then, the issue is how the repair time for the next asset might be reduced. Once the backlog of due-outs for a given NIIN is eliminated, the important factor becomes the responsiveness to the next demand. Therefore, we are concerned with both lead-time reduction for the next repair and reduction in overall repair flow time.

In the M88A1 case, it is possible that some of the WIP, which remained at approximately 70 engines during our analysis, could be used to shorten the achievable repair lead time for the next engine from weeks to days or even hours. To achieve such reductions, an analysis and strategy must be developed for each NIIN considered. Decisions must be made concerning the desired level of WIP necessary to buffer each repair activity or step. The logic works backward from the final action of the repair cycle, based on the desired marginal repair-time goal (i.e., the typical lead time until the next asset will be available for issue). The times and variability experienced for each step in the repair of an item, along with the marginal repair-time goal, help define the size of the buffer at each step and the total WIP for that NIIN. That total defines the expected minimum WIP to support current repair activities while achieving the desired repair lead time.[3]

For the M88A1 engine, we developed an alternative that would enable the next repair to be completed, on average, in one work shift. Some would consider this improvement to be quite responsive, while others might say that the process needs to be even faster or that the capacity needs to be more than just the next engine. Other options could improve responsiveness still more. For example, an engine could be already completed, awaiting the signal to call DLA for pickup, or two or more fully assembled WIP engines could be held in a condition ready to send to testing. Reparable management concerns thousands of different items of differing repair complexity and technology. The applicability of any given improvement alternative should be evaluated on a NIIN-by-NIIN basis.

By "working backward" through the repair activities, one could determine how much partially repaired WIP should be positioned before each activity to enable the subsequent activity to respond to the completion of the next engine. This would then

---

[3] For this discussion, we have assumed an ultimate goal of small-batch or even single-item production activity at each step of the repair process. Technology and other production factors may argue for larger batch sizes, but this does not change the basic logic of the argument. The object is to reduce lead time to improve response to customer needs.

ripple through the completion of all the replacement components in the total repair flow. In other words, as an engine is shipped, just enough WIP would be pulled forward to replace the assembled engine, then all the components and parts necessary for the assembly, and so on. The level of buffering inventory required in front of each activity would depend on the processing time of that activity with respect to the processing times and capacities of the activities before and after it and the maximum repair-production rate desired.

The system already typically contains considerable WIP, so any WIP above the levels determined for each of the buffers across the flow would be a target for reduction. However, by starting at the end of the process to draw down excess WIP, a depot might also prevent the expenditure of time and materials on assets that are not required. For example, a depot generally does not want to induct an unserviceable asset into repair and consume resources ahead of the lead time necessary to meet production schedules and requests for serviceables.

Therefore, in addition to lead-time reduction, it is also important to consider overall repair flow times, preventing wasted repair actions in WIP, and achieving efficiency by reducing overall WIP consistent with defined responsiveness goals.

Frequent Replanning to Keep Repairs Synchronized with Demand

A similar pull production technique can be used to adjust repair levels in response to changing customer demands.

Capacity and priorities help planners arrange production schedules and solve problems that can arise in matching the workload with the available workforce. At the work-center level, tasks are often variable or changing, as the workload is usually characterized by multiple PRONs for multiple different items of similar technology. Thus, the shop that repairs the M88A1 engine also repairs several other diesel engines of various sizes and complexity, the major accessory components for those engines, and transmissions and other heavy mechanical parts. The equipment, tools, and technical skills needed for these jobs are similar, and the aggregate workload provides a sufficient total workload volume to support this capacity, as well as enough variety to keep the workforce engaged when one item hits a bottleneck.

However, frequent replanning is needed to keep the number and type of repairs synchronized with changing demands—and thus to ensure that the depot repair process is responsive to customer needs. The current RD&ES module receives monthly information that can be used to revise production schedules for the currently approved PRON.

A new set of operating practices is also needed that will enable the depot production to respond to this improved forecast, preferably one that would not require any additional software or modifications to existing programs and would be easy to communicate among all those involved. Depot technicians who had been around when the workload for the M88A1 engine was much higher described such a method during our walk-through of the current process. The method was very similar to Toyota's *kanban* system and the lean manufacturing approach.[4]

This alternative involves a pull production technique similar to that described in the discussion of lead-time reduction, in which a mechanism or signal communicates to workers the need to perform a given task and the quantity to be produced. The initial signal might be triggered by the final step in a process, such as a DLA pickup of finished containers or the movement of assembled engines to the test facility. This step would signal the pull on the production flow. The final action controlled by the scheduler at the work center thus becomes the signal that flows backward through the facility as each activity responds in turn to the movement of an asset from the completed WIP pile. In other words, the empty space on the floor is the authorization for a worker to induct material into the activity and produce the replacement to fill the space.[5]

As simple as it sounds, such a system can be very effective for production control. The process proposed here would extend a system of linked signals back up the production flow to ensure the availability of parts necessary to sustain the responsiveness of the marginal repair-time goal. Because this is not a continuous production line, nor are all the required activities performed in the same facility, a system of signals would need to be developed for each NIIN.

After linking the IM to the repair-shop scheduler and the scheduler to the pull signal, the other supporting activities could work off the signals on the critical repair flow path. For example, containers of unserviceable engines awaiting induction could be staged in small batches at the facility. An engine would not be inducted until the technician received the signal to induct one, but larger and more-economical delivery lots from bulk storage would still be possible. Similar adjustments would be possible

---

[4] A *kanban*, or signal, is the mechanism used in many manufacturing plants to communicate to workers the need to perform a given task and the quantity or batch size to be produced. The *kanban* is a key feature of pull production systems: As material moves forward, the worker typically, in turn, automatically trips a *kanban* upstream (i.e., uses positioned material, exposes an empty position, or reserved material location) that causes a task to occur. That task then positions material in anticipation of the next downstream pull signal. Each signal sets off a ripple of upstream actions that pull just enough material forward through the production process. These signal systems are usually very low-tech and have very small batch sizes. Thus they are inexpensive to implement, and they minimize inventory investment.

[5] The *kanban* system is very much like the system used by ANAD technicians in the past. The mechanic in the assembly area required a set of matched items (with matched dimensions) to proceed with assembly. The assembly technician pulled the components from their prepositioned locations on a large shadow board (where every component had a unique location) as he proceeded with the initial assembly. When the partial assembly was moved to the next workstation, the empty shadow board was moved away and the technician checked to see if he was to start another assembly or shift to a different task. If he was to do another assembly, another shadow board was preloaded and waiting to be moved into position. An indirect labor technician took the empty shadow board to the upstream activities to reload it for a future assembly.

The shadow board was the *kanban*, or signal, that linked these activities. The immediate upstream activity took measurements and collected just enough sets of matched components to restock the shadow board. Once the board was restocked, the technician switched to other necessary tasks in the work center.

for reclaimed components, large quantities of which (both serviceable and unserviceable) were in the facility on our visits. The signal system could be expanded to use the Automated Storage and Retrieval System (ASRS) facility as a remote buffer location. This would free up storage space in the production facility, and the ASRS automation could be used to track levels of inventory and dispatch material for processing as necessary. The ASRS can aid the shop schedulers in seeing the WIP and determining where it is located.

As the shop controls for each NSN transition to a pull-signal approach, some simple rules will be needed to enable a technician to make a decision when more than one signal is present. In practice, this is not a serious problem, because the decision is ultimately linked to the specific lead time required to support the tasks that are pulling the material.

Improving the Availability of Unserviceable Assets

Because a repair action cannot begin until an unserviceable is available for induction, and because unserviceables are often the source of critical repair parts, it is important to ensure that unserviceable assets are available when needed. Currently, unserviceables (unless specially identified) are treated as the lowest-priority items in both supply and transportation activities. The priority given to dealing with unserviceable assets should be reevaluated so that they can better be used to address the needs of customers requesting reparables and the Army as a whole.

To help in understanding how this process might be improved, Figure 5.2 shows a generalized view of the reverse logistics process, that is, the way an unserviceable gets to the required location to support reparable activities.[6]

As shown at the left side of the figure, an unserviceable is typically removed from an end-item being repaired. Traceable metrics are available today only from the point at which the item is first turned in to tactical-level supply. Because unserviceables are usually given the lowest priority, the retrograde flow for unserviceable items is much slower than that for serviceables.

In part to motivate prompt turn-in of unserviceables, payment for assets was imposed in 1992. The unit receives a credit (reducing the total effective cost) when it returns an unserviceable to supply. However, shifting credit rates have left customers uncertain of refund amounts or about whether they will receive a refund at all. Thus, the Army VM analysis showed slow times and episodic patterns for turn-ins and credit payments.[7]

---

[6] A more detailed discussion of reverse logistics within the Army can be found in Diener et al., 2004.

[7] In April 1992, the Army changed its financial system for DLRs. Prior to that time, AMC received appropriated funds to procure and repair DLRs, which were issued as direct issue to logistics customers, based on their stated needs. Other types of spare parts (i.e., FLRs and consumables) had previously been stock-funded; thus, stock-funding DLRs brought all types of spare parts under the same type of financial system.

Figure 5.2
Generalized Reverse Logistics Process

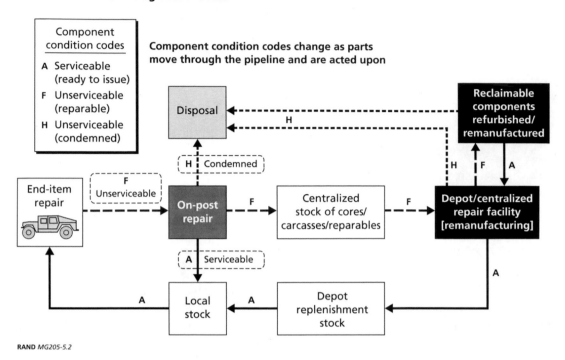

This pattern has not been readily apparent for some older equipment that had sufficient reparable assets in national stock after the post–Cold War force-structure drawdown. However, the problem has recently been emerging more frequently. For some new systems and some older systems with modernized components, the total depth of stock is inadequate to cushion the impact of slow retrograde. Furthermore, slow retrograde has delayed implementation of more-aggressive condemnation policies for some older components. Therefore, concerns about improving retrograde flows have arisen in the Army for the same basic reasons they appeared earlier in the Air Force and the Navy.

As Army maintenance is transformed toward rearward consolidation of component repair, more importance will be placed on time-sensitive repair of reparable assets to place serviceable items on the shelf for the next customer demand. The Air Force has demonstrated the capability to achieve consistent total broken-to-fixed reparable cycle times of less than 30 days for some items.[8] The commercial sector has

---

[8] The depot repair enhancement process (DREP) is governed by Air Force Materiel Command Instruction (AFMCI) 21-129. The Air Force view of reparable repair includes reduced flow days, a focus on constraint management, improvements to management systems that provide daily prioritization of repairs, improved supply support to the repair shops, alignment of responsibility and authority of key players, and customer-driven performance measures at the depot (e.g., item BO rates, CWT, retrograde time). DREP concepts apply to both or-

achieved these levels or better, nationally and internationally, for high-value computer and medical-equipment component remanufacturing, and even for selected diesel-engine components.[9]

Both the supply community and the transportation community need to review the priorities given to unserviceable assets, which can be the source of fill for the next customer demand or replenishment action. "Saving" resources with policies that will soon necessitate costly expediting and workarounds can be wasteful to the overall Army logistics system.

Improving the Process for Managing Repair Parts

Lack of parts to support repair-process activities is one of the most often reported limitations on responsive repair. Our case-study evidence supported this claim. The parts used in repairs of the type we are concerned with generally fall into two categories, reclaimed parts and new parts.[10] Unserviceable items are disassembled, cleaned, and inspected with the aim of reusing as much of the materiel as is practical.[11] Parts that cannot be salvaged are replaced with new ones. Theoretically, every part has a probability of being reclaimable, given certain conditions of wear or damage. On occasion, parts that are generally thought of as reclaimable must be replaced by new ones.

During the process walk-through, we discovered that the problems with repair parts availability have two aspects: the controls on the availability of parts at the work locations and the adequacy of the supporting inventory policy. Both these issues must be addressed in order to improve the process for managing spare parts.

Availability and Control of Parts

The current process of getting needed parts to mechanics and keeping shop supply rooms adequately stocked is less than effective in supporting a responsive repair process. When a technician needs parts for a repair action, he or she typically leaves the work location and goes to the shop supply room to get whatever is needed. However, experienced mechanics are expensive assets, and their time is wasted when they go to the stockroom individually to pick up parts. Moreover, this system makes it difficult

---

ganic and contractor-repaired assets. John Stone at Warner-Robins Air Logistics Center provided examples of implementation progress.

[9] The authors observed this level of performance at FedEx Logistics repair operations in Memphis and Cummins operations in Indianapolis.

[10] Another category of parts, bench stock, refers to the common, low-cost hardware and housekeeping items found in any shop. Technically, these are new parts, but because they are typically inexpensive and readily available, they are seldom the cause of nonresponsiveness.

[11] While various activities are performed on these reclaimable items, the items are typically considered to be in WIP. Whether a reclaimable item or an end-item is being repaired, the material is viewed as WIP inventory from induction until a final state is reached (i.e., serviceable or condemned).

for stockroom clerks to keep track of inventory. For example, at ANAD, no record was made of materiel that mechanics obtained on a self-service basis from the supply rooms. A stockroom clerk checked inventory weekly and sent weekly (as well as emergency) requests to the scheduling clerk for the applicable PRON. The scheduling clerk worked from the production schedule, using a manual analysis to verify that sufficient parts were on hand in the stockroom and the ASRS to cover the next 60 days of scheduled production. The scheduling clerk submitted replenishment requests for the stockroom online and had a separate interface to the installation supply account (ISA) to requisition additional stock for the ASRS. The ISA inventory was recently eliminated from the repair depots; however, the ISA computer is still used to generate requisitions for replenishment from the source of supply. The computer processes the scheduling clerk's requisition to the Defense Automated Addressing System (DAAS) and the appropriate inventory control point (ICP) for sourcing instructions in a manner like that used to process a tactical-level customer's requisition through the SARSS.

Almost all reclaimed items flow through their necessary repair actions and return directly to the shop stockroom. Depending upon the total materiel in WIP, the quantity of reclaimed items may vary and can amount to more than 60 days' stock. Extensive man-hours are invested in tracking down reclaimable WIP that has not reached the stockroom when needed.[12] A similar pattern exists for backordered new piece parts (for both Army- and DLA-managed items).

In an effort to make the repair parts system more responsive, we offer the following suggestions, which we discussed with personnel at ANAD.

Control access to the shop supply room and issue parts at the mechanic work-stations. Materiel should be available to mechanics at their work locations. Under this approach, the clerk issues parts from the room and therefore is in a position to pick parts and note the need for restocking on a single pass at a location, meaning that the weekly inventory and order submission would no longer be required. This change would improve decisionmaking by increasing the frequency of reviews and eliminating the opportunity for an item to go to zero balance before a reorder is placed. As this process is implemented, the mechanic and the supply room clerk can determine together the total quantity of each NSN that will be needed at a given workstation for planned increments of work. A parts list might also be built for each workstation that would enable the mechanic to easily request restock quantities periodically.

Look for opportunities to assemble kits of new and reclaimed parts. The automation in the ASRS can be used to help prepare kits for some or all of the parts

---

[12] On several different visits to the case-study work center, we noted both mechanics and indirect labor engaged in these efforts. Managers told us that this was a common, recurring problem.

required at workstations where repetitive assembly actions take place.[13] ASRS currently responds to the shop stock room within about 24 hours of an online request for material by the scheduling clerk. The items in the ASRS are owned by maintenance (i.e., this is "issued" materiel or shop stock that is not reflected on supply inventory records anywhere); they include WIP assemblies, reclaimed materiel, new piece parts, and other material staged to support modification and overhaul programs at the depot. The ASRS capability also supports "kitting" of materiel in support of depot tasks. At ANAD, the ASRS is housed within a separate building, but at most other depots, the ASRS is within the main maintenance facility.

This approach would cut out the stockroom inventory layer for many items and could link inventories more closely to actual production. For example, if a mechanic is scheduled to assemble two "widgets" per day, the scheduler could pull two kits per day forward from the ASRS (which has an inherent kit-building capability) and buffer the process with an additional prepositioned kit. Any unused parts could be returned to the ASRS inventory for future kits.

Modify the routing of reclaimed parts. The repair process would also benefit from changes in the procedures for routing reclaimed parts.[14] During one case-study visit, we noticed that there were frequent delays in the process used to batch reclaimed items so that they could be routed appropriately. At the time, reclaimed parts were sorted into metal tote baskets with similar materiel; after each basket was filled, it was routed through a sequence of work centers where each item was cleaned, repaired, plated, machined, or painted, as necessary, depending upon its specifications. The size of the batch was typically determined by how much of the material fit into the standard tote. To minimize set-up time (e.g., for painting), work centers along the individual item routings often batch processed totes of several different items that required common applications in that work center. If an item was large, the tote filled quickly after a few unserviceables were disassembled, allowing it to be routed fairly quickly. The tote for small items, however, could sit for an extended period until enough carcasses were disassembled to generate sufficient materiel to fill the tote. The focus on the efficiency of large batches was driving total WIP.

By routing reclaimable material frequently in small batches and on a daily basis, personnel could capitalize on common routings of items by placing them into the same tote. During a subsequent visit, we learned that another depot activity that was

---

[13] The elimination of the ISA inventory and warehouse removed a whole level of inventory between the ASRS and the DLA distribution center located at each Army maintenance depot. It also eliminated the civilian supply manpower. DLA stocks items at collocated distribution centers on the basis of local demand history and usually delivers locally issued material to ASRS within 24 hours of the MRO. The distribution center also stocks serviceable and unserviceable Army-managed items as directed by an IM. At ANAD, significant DLA space is dedicated to unserviceable-asset storage. DLA also currently provides the few supply specialists necessary to operate the warehousing tasks at the ASRS facility on a reimbursable basis.

[14] This procedure has since begun to change, in part, as will be explained later.

working with a contractor to improve the reclaimed-materiel routing and tracking process had begun to implement such a procedure.[15] The contractor linked the change in the routing process to the automation of the bill of materials associated with the depot maintenance work requirement (DMWR) and bar coding, which helped generate automated routing documents and track progress by reading the bar code during the actual materiel flow. During subsequent visits to the facility, we observed the pilot implementation, and the impact of these new procedures was evident. The schedulers and shop floor managers reported immediate improvements in the visibility of WIP materials, and, more important, they quickly saw that the smaller batch sizes provided a steady flow of reclaimed materiel to the assembly areas, reducing the need for expedited actions.

Route reclaimed parts to the ASRS. The final destination for all the reclaimed-parts routing orders should be the ASRS, since input to the ASRS changes the recorded inventory quantity for the part and records the storage location, both of which are visible to schedulers and other depot managers. All parts, whether reclaimed or new, can then be brought forward in an orderly manner as required to support production.

For example, routing reclaimable materiel from a disassembled carcass can lead to a net growth in inventory of some reclaimed items if it is not tracked well. In the case-study PRON, a total of 70 engines were inducted and in various states of WIP. These engines had each been removed from the shipping container and disassembled into piece parts for cleaning and inspection. The parts are interchangeable and not readily associated with the originally inducted, serial-numbered asset. If a separate PRON for the same NIIN were released, calling for the disassembly of the engines to reclaim certain parts that were in short supply, the rest of the unserviceable parts would be scrapped, because there would be a net excess of unserviceable carcasses. Without tight shop-floor controls, unintended reclaiming of parts would be possible. When the parts remain on the work floor without WIP accountability and visibility,

---

[15] The contractor, Robbins-Gioia, Inc., had a multitask contract, which focused on consolidating data generated through the various legacy data systems at the depot into an integrated database. The contractor then developed and exploited tools for mining that data for direct applications that address the needs of working-level managers. These contractor engineers and IT specialists had expertise that was not available at ANAD (partly because training programs were not available). For the reclaimed-parts routing task, the contractor developed a bill-of-materials routing flow based on the depot-maintenance work requirement (DMWR) for each reparable NIIN. The DMWR was found to be significantly outdated with respect to current task activities for many parts. These errors are not important in the accuracy of documentation, but the delays, misroutings, and lost materiel cause increased costs and delayed production.

The implementation of improvements in reclaimed-parts routing and tracking was a pilot effort limited to the materiel flowing from a single NSN repair program. It will require significant time and work to expand this to other items and other work centers. The contractor has shared its expertise, but the depot has not yet trained its workers to continue the expansion of this effort on their own. An IT investment was also required to permit bar-code scanning for tracking materiel flow during repair. We do not know whether these capabilities are incorporated in the Logistics Modernization Program (LMP) IT upgrade that is now under way.

it is very difficult to be sure how many of each piece part are actually on hand. The ASRS provides both efficient storage and inventory visibility.

Use pull production techniques to reduce batch sizes and WIP inventory. As pull production scheduling and small-batch routing of reclaimable materiel is implemented across the facility for each NSN type, opportunities to reduce WIP will emerge. The number of WIP engines in the case study (70) should be reduced over time. The optimal number is not known at this time, but the desired state would be the point at which waste has been reduced so that a demand signal causes an induction that leads to a complete repair the same day. Such a radically different end-state can hardly be imagined today for this engine, even though for most reparable workload, the total time required for all the value-adding actions amounts to only minutes or hours. The elimination of waste eliminates the need for buffer inventory and dramatically improves responsiveness.

National Inventory Policy

The management of repair parts can also be improved by the policy used to determine inventory levels of reclaimed parts and new piece parts. Reclaimed parts typically have a "washout" or condemnation rate, since not all used materiel can be successfully returned to satisfactory condition. Therefore, it is important to know when a washout occurs so that new replacement materiel will be available to complete the subsequent assembly or repair action.

New piece parts are the greatest policy challenge. They can vary in cost from a few cents to tens of thousands of dollars, and a single reparable item might potentially consume several hundred of them for a single repair. The issue of new piece parts in particular raises the question of how the Army depots can support the repairs required to meet customer demands while keeping inventory investment to a minimum.

The diversity in the number, cost, and complexity of parts needed for different repairs means that a single rule or policy for determining how many of each item to stock in inventory to support the expected repair programs is not likely to achieve either effectiveness or efficiency. Unfortunately, the current policies and practices for managing repair-parts inventory frequently result in stock outages and consequent work stoppages. It is therefore necessary to examine how much should be invested, by item, and where the items should be positioned to support the repair operation.

The basic inventory policy for new piece parts at AMC maintenance depots, 60 days of supply (DOS), applies to all items other than bench stock and special-project assets. But an investment of 60 DOS is too high for many items and not nearly sufficient to prevent work stoppages and workarounds for others. The intent of the current policy is to have the last of the repair parts used as the depot finishes the approved PRON, thus minimizing parts investment and the risk that a PRON might not be approved for the next period for the same NSN. However, many repair programs will be renewed yearly for the foreseeable future, so this policy increases the risk of nonresponsive repair at the beginning of a recurring PRON in the coming year.[16]

Clearly, it will be difficult to address inventory investment policies until some aspects of inventory control are improved, but it is not premature to make some observations and propose some alternatives.

Use demand as the primary indicator for repair-part inventory planning. The traditional AMC policy, which codes the requisitions for parts supporting reparable PRONs as nonrecurring demands, is contrary to the needs of both the repair depot and the IMs. Reparable assets are intended to be repaired on a recurring basis over the lifetime of the end-item they support. These are not nonrecurring modifications or other special depot-level projects, which also occur in the overall maintenance-depot workload.

Both AMC policy and the repair depot's ISA should be changed to code all repair-part requests supporting recurring reparable programs as recurring demands. That coding would provide immediate feedback to the managing national inventory-control point (NICP) about the true nature of usage for each piece part. Information on nonrecurring coded transactions does not flow automatically in the same manner. However, in an attempt to provide better support, DLA has ensured that NSNs ordered at least four times are treated as recurring, even when the requisitions are coded "nonrecurring." It is important to ensure that the NICP gets correct information about asset usage so that inventory and vendor relationships can be maintained. The current procedures introduce a lag of six to 18 months (and sometimes more) in the feedback about demand.

The current procedure, called the parts-explosion process (PEP), was intended to express the future demand expectations for depot repair parts to both Army and DLA IMs. Some believe that the current PEP is too slow to provide responsive feedback and too error-prone to be trusted by the IMs. They refer to the lack of willingness by AMC to fund inventory-investment projections based on the PEP as partial evidence to support this conclusion. We traced the PEP procedures for the M88A1 engine repair at ANAD and found that the information on quantities or repair parts used and the probabilities of use per repair are aggregated at the completion of a PRON. The data are collected for each PRON. If a PRON is judged by the TACOM depot-maintenance managers to be nonrepresentative workload, those data are ignored. The resulting "valid" data are used to update the PEP model that recommends the parts necessary to support the future PRON then under development.

---

[16] This discussion follows the basic logic that it is important to bring the existing inventories and supply practices under control before undertaking additional investment. However, during the course of the case study, we noted that some individual items were clearly stocked in insufficient quantity. Therefore, inventory-policy alternatives will also be discussed below.

The intent is to provide advance notification to the NICPs of repair-part requirements for that forthcoming PRON. However, the parts usage is not aggregated until a PRON is completed, and the information is not provided to the NICP until the PRON workload forecast is to be approved, 12 to 18 months in the future. Furthermore, both TACOM and DLA personnel involved with the case study reported that the PEP recommendations were not good predictions of actual future demands. Therefore, DLA will not use the PEP as the basis for inventory investment unless the Army obligates its funds in advance. TACOM has not done that. We were shown the most recent PEP output that was sent to DLA. Using an audit program that reviews the information for glaring errors (e.g., a forecast of 100,000 for a low-use item), DLA had identified more than 40 percent of the item recommendations as probable errors. The PEP is complex, delays the availability of useful feedback, and does not provide the desired results. In the meantime, parts use continues daily and valid use data could be provided automatically to the NICPs to help guide their inventory planning.[17]

Depot-Level Inventory Policy

The preceding discussion concerns national-level inventory decisions. An improved inventory-decision policy is also needed to buffer the demands at the repair locations, the repair depots.

Adopt a variable repair-parts-inventory policy to allow for greater diversity. The current policies and practices determining the size of the inventory investment and the optimum location for positioning inventory evolved in response to pressures to reduce investment. To achieve that goal, whole levels of inventory were eliminated and maximum DOS was specified for individual items (i.e., elimination of the ISA).

However, the critical issue is not the DOS on hand; it is the assurance that replenishment of shop stocks is readily available. An inventory policy should not just limit investment in repair inventory, it should also provide a clear signal to IMs about the usage or consumption of inventory items. Thus, the reorder point for shop stock generally needs to be close enough to the inventory objective level that reorders of relatively small amounts occur frequently. For example, future IT improvements should include point-of-sale data collection that feeds parts-consumption data directly to supply managers so that the automated decision-support tools will replenish and adjust inventory levels throughout the supply chain to achieve the desired results.

The policy should also allow for more diversity to address the different characteristics of individual repair parts. We suggest that it should at least distinguish

---

[17] The PEP has a logical basis. Detailed data on part failures and consumption encountered during asset repair can be very valuable for reliability analyses of both reparable assets and problem piece parts. However, improvement of reparable-assets reliability is beyond the scope of this research. It is possible that elements of the PEP could provide critical information.

among items used for nearly all repairs, items used less frequently, items that are used infrequently and have long lead times for replenishment, and items that are used infrequently and have short lead times for replenishment.

Frequently used items. The largest group of new repair parts comprises the items that are used for nearly all the repairs performed for a given NSN—both new items from vendors and subordinate reparables, which can be repaired either by the government or by a contractor. As long as these items are produced and available on a monthly basis, replenishment under the current 60-DOS policy should provide a demand history that can be used by the PRON IM and the repair-parts IM to ensure that assets are on hand and that there is a continuing vendor relationship to meet future needs. Both DLA and the Army should position such items at the local DLA distribution center and/or the appropriate regional strategic distribution platform (SDP) (i.e., Susquehanna (DDSP) or San Joaquin (DDJC)) to provide replenishment at a defined CWT from the scheduling clerk's request.

Eventually, the scheduling clerk should be able to improve the 60-day level to 45 days and then to 30 days, with no degradation in support but with the appropriate one-time savings in inventory investment (i.e., up to half the average inventory value of the 60-DOS policy). However, given the low dollar amount tied up in this inventory, it is probably not prudent to begin with such an emphasis on efficiency. Instead, retention of the current 60-DOS policy during initial implementation can ensure that the depot is comfortable with the level of risk. The achieved CWT and its variability should determine the final inventory depth for frequently used items.

The actual cost of these items should also factor into this decision, because some of them are inexpensive and basic economic order quantity (EOQ) logic may be appropriate. Because the cost for the clerk to order via the ISA should be very low, the economic leverage should favor smaller order quantities.

Less frequently used items. A different policy could apply to those items used less frequently. It is important to ensure that multiple replenishments of these items occur during a year and that the IM has stock on hand and a current vendor relationship. The risk of stock-out is greatest in cases when there have been infrequent replenishments, the IM is nearly out of stock, and a new procurement will need to be undertaken. When this risk is relatively high, 60 DOS will not likely be enough, given the lead time of the replenishment and procurement activities. Frequent shop-replenishment orders signal the DLA system (for example) that there is an active demand for the item, thus indicating that DLA should maintain stock and a vendor relationship for prompt replenishment. The PRON IM should work with the depot's scheduling clerk and the repair-parts IMs supporting the PRON for such items to ensure that assets and vendor sources are available.

Infrequently used long-lead-time items. A different policy is required for parts that are used infrequently and that have long lead times for replenishment, i.e., items that are no longer manufactured for the commercial market and for which the depot is virtually the sole remaining customer. The government is often forced to buy more of such items than it would normally want in the near term to justify the setup costs for a one-time manufacture by a vendor. These items typically are a small percentage of the total items, but they can account for a majority of the total inventory investment. Thus, they require and justify intensive management. We found several examples of such items during our case study. The diesel-engine block, crankshaft, and cylinder heads were seldom condemned during their first 20 years or so. However, the engine used in the M88A1 vehicle has now been out of production for more than 20 years, and wear and fatigue appear to be taking a toll. Years ago, engineers and supply specialists anticipated the need to buy spares for these critical components and made the necessary investment. Now the time has come to replenish those stocks, but unfortunately, the original manufacturer is no longer producing them and is not interested in working a one-time order into its production schedule. As a result, the lead time to replace these items in inventory is now years instead of months.

The circumstances are not always so extreme. Long lead times are driven by setup and manufacturing in addition to the more complex acquisition process itself. The PRON IM and the depot need to identify long-lead-time items and take action to assure availability long before the repair technician asks for the last part on the shelf. For such cases, no mere DOS policy is relevant. The good news is that there are relatively few long-lead-time items for each PRON, and in some cases, extraordinary workarounds exist for completing repairs without difficult-to-acquire parts. Such workarounds and the investment required to keep needed parts available are simply two of the costs of doing business.[18]

Infrequently used short-lead-time items. The policy for infrequently used short-lead-time items is simple. As long as the lead time remains short, there is no reason to invest in more than the minimal inventory. However, care must be taken to assure that these NSNs remain available.

Use workarounds as an inventory policy of last resort. When the existing policies of any maintenance system fail to provide adequate materiel, all levels of the system (in the Army, a sister service, or a commercial operation) develop alternative methods or workarounds to meet the requirements. Several well-recognized workarounds are in use at the repair depots. The criticality of the customer's need is relevant when determining whether or not a particular alternative should be applied, and some "necessary" workarounds could be made less difficult and less expensive for the depot—and ultimately, the Army.

---

[18] The fact that a given item was designated as reparable rather than disposable was the result of an earlier decision analysis to either repair or buy upon failure. The analysis is usually called LORA (level-of-repair analysis) and could be repeated throughout the life cycle of the system if desired. However, given the decision to repair an item, the repair parts must be available in time to support the repair turnaround concept that is chosen. The number of reparable items assumes a given turnaround concept, including repair-process timing.

Exchanging Parts Among Unserviceables

One common form of workaround, the "rob back," can provide parts necessary to complete a repair but can also lead to an accumulation of WIP. A rob back is a form of controlled substitution or cannibalization of parts from one assembly to repair another. The need to cannibalize parts appears to be one of the main motivations for the induction of large batches of unserviceables. The resulting WIP material becomes an inventory of potential parts that can be swapped and robbed to continue production of serviceable assets. However, the practice has its limitations. For example, even though the WIP for the M88A1 stood at approximately 70 engines, there were no items left to rob for some critical parts. In other words, the repair process was short 70 each of at least one repair part. This condition may be temporary and may be associated with replenishment due-in from a vendor or with a bottleneck in processing reclaimable materiel. The inventory-control improvements discussed earlier would help to prevent unnecessary rob backs due to misplaced WIP.

Scavenging Parts from Condemned Assets

Another type of workaround involves disassembly for parts of long-lead-time or condemned end-items. Assets for this purpose have become increasingly available in recent years due to the general drawdown in force structure within the Army. For example, the number of M88A1s in the inventory has been reduced, so the number of spare engines has been comparatively reduced, and the number of unserviceable assets is determined to exceed expected future needs. Given the long lead times needed to acquire certain critical repair parts, the decision has been made at the IM staff level to disassemble some number of unserviceable assets to recover or reclaim certain critical assets.[19] The value of these excess engines is a sunk cost and is therefore irrelevant to the decision. The reclaimed parts cost the man-hours and processing to return them to serviceable condition. This can easily be less than the cost of the new repair parts from a vendor. What must be guarded against is the potential for growth in WIP for items that are not needed but are the by-product of the disassembly process. The inventory-control improvements discussed earlier relate directly to this issue.

Local Purchase

Another type of workaround is the local purchase of assets not available in time through the normal supply-management procedures. In the case study, the procedures required to complete normal supply-management actions were much more complicated and drawn out than those seen at most Army installations and motor

---

[19] In this case, the IM developed a separate PRON to tear down some of the unserviceables in storage for parts. This PRON became an alternative to the long-lead-time parts-procurement alternative discussed above for these items.

pools. The documentation and processing of one transaction at the depot took more than 30 days, while the tactical motor pool could have taken a credit card to a local merchant to obtain the same part the same day. But while the prompt local purchase of material can be an important alternative course of action, drastically simplified procedures are needed for situations where material is available locally from commercial sources. For example, in the case in question, the item costs were less than $10 each and the total purchase was less than $100, so the cost to the depot for lost production and processing far exceeded the purchase price.

Heroic Efforts

Sometimes, because of a critical need, heroic efforts are made to reclaim material from a carcass that would, under normal conditions, be condemned and disposed of. This is a valuable service for certain critical materials. In such cases, a mechanic must ensure that quality standards are maintained and must often make several attempts before obtaining a serviceable item. Thus, the cost of these workarounds can be high and quite variable. However, the practice is profitable enough that it has attracted entrepreneurs to DLA disposal sites to buy such "junk" and salvage parts that are then sold back to the government.

The expense of workaround procedures can range from trivial for the rob back of a single item that was disassembled anyway to extensive man-hours of rework; the benefit can be the prevention of idle manpower and facilities due to a work stoppage. These costs and benefits, along with other relevant data, need to be factored into the inventory investment-decision equation.

Financial Policies That Support More-Responsive Depot Repairs

Adopt financial policies that encourage more-efficient depot repair. There are two areas in which financial policy appears to be a negative issue limiting the responsiveness of repair activities: (1) the carryover of workload of approved PRONs into months of the next fiscal year, and (2) the need to align cost allocations to more accurately reflect the cost of repair activities and to price reparable assets as an incentive to field managers to make the best purchase-versus-repair decisions for the Army. Decisions based on local optimization are often at odds with the most economically favorable decision for the Army.

Adopt policies that make repair programs responsive to customer demands. The current yearly PRON approval process encourages carryover of workload from one year to the next. The Army maintenance depots' component-repair programs are financed via the AWCF, a revolving fund, rather than direct congressional appropriations. Unlike congressionally approved budgets, revolving-fund activities are not required to spend all their funds by the end of the fiscal year to avoid losing the money. Thus, depots carry over workload beyond its intended fiscal year to provide cash flow for labor and materiel to support approved PRONs.

Since the congressional budget is almost never approved before October 1, new PRONs are not approved for release at the start of the fiscal year, and the depot cannot begin them on time. In fact, the depot cannot even order parts to preposition them against a new PRON. Therefore, workload carryover can complicate the timely meeting of customer demands when the approved PRON quantity was consistent with actual demands through the end of the completed fiscal year.[20]

Repair depots have learned this lesson, so they plan to carry over work from the previous PRON to keep the workforce busy. This stretching of the production schedule happens yearly, and the normal expectation is that the depot will not have a released PRON for the current fiscal year until December or January.

A 2001 GAO report[21] addressed the funding issues associated with stretching depot workload from one year to the next. The GAO found that DoD had not documented an analytical basis for its three-month carryover practice and that, without such analysis, there can be no assurance of a smooth transition from one fiscal year to the next and no measure of whether the carryover is sufficient or excessive. The report further identifies specific problems in Army depot maintenance:

> The actual reported year-end carryover for Army's depot maintenance and ordnance activity groups exceeded the 3-month carryover standard consistently from fiscal year 1996 through fiscal year 2000.

For fiscal year 2000, Army officials stated that there were four reasons that the actual reported year-end carryover balance exceeded the standard and budget projections:

- Some depots could not obtain the parts needed in a timely manner, so that less work was performed than planned.
- Some depots did not accurately estimate the time and resources needed to complete jobs.
- Emergency situations, such as unplanned orders to perform safety-of-flight work, delayed work on orders already accepted by the depots.
- The composition and size of the workload changed from the budget projections due to changes in customer funding and priorities (GAO, 2001b, pp. 14–15).

Workload carryover and the pattern of delayed production, along with changes in demand, contribute to the due-out volume and the BO rate. The Army needs to revise policies to reconcile its current contradictory financial incentives and to ensure

---

[20] DoD and Army financial policy (as currently interpreted) prevents repair managers from starting the new PRON. However, the number of repairs authorized under the previous PRON could potentially be adjusted to reflect the actual sales (and the necessary repairs). That is not the current practice. (See also footnote 11 in Chapter Three.)

[21] GAO, 2001b.

that customer demands are met promptly. The new policy must enable the workforce to be paid while customers continue placing demands funded by a continuing resolution covering mission activities that the continuing resolution supports.

Align cost and pricing to reflect the cost of repairs to the Army. Changes in the Army's budgeting, price, and credit policies have a particularly strong influence on the behavior of logistics customers because those customers make purchasing, inventory, repair, and turn-in decisions based on the budgets they receive and the prices and credits they face. Depot repair is affected by several current Army financial policies, including the implementation of transfer pricing (AWCF), the lack of direct funding for fixed costs, and the lack of exchange pricing, under which requests and returns can be combined into one financial transaction.[22]

The Army's current financing system was intended to provide incentives to both logistics suppliers and customers to maintain the Army's weapon systems cost-effectively—for suppliers to reduce costs, and for customers to use resources wisely. In 1992, DoD implemented stock funding of DLRs in an effort to gain the effects of free markets. This resulted in logistics customers being given budgets to buy supplies and repairs from Army or DoD logistics suppliers. Under this market-like mechanism, customers pay for items they order and receive credits for items they return. Tactical- and national-level inventories are financed by stock funds, and suppliers must replenish these inventories with income from sales net of credits to make the stock funds ultimately break even.[23]

Customer behavior has a strong influence on the cash and materiel inflows and outflows of the Army's stock funds and thus on their solvency. Customers may seek the best price for costly items and may therefore purchase these items from a source other than the supply system. The supply system then loses a "sale," and revenue or cash flow needed by the stock fund is not realized.

The prices of Army-managed items are set at the latest acquisition cost (LAC) or latest repair cost (LRC) plus a supply-management surcharge to recover the costs of operating the wholesale supply system.[24] Even if the Army's LAC is low because it is able to make volume buys, the surcharge acts as a "tax" on purchases from the supply system. When items have commercial equivalents, customers are likely to choose the least-expensive alternative, if it is easily available. Even when the Army's acquisition cost is lower than local vendors' prices, a high surcharge may make local purchase the

---

[22] This discussion draws upon earlier RAND work and is presented to explicitly address the linkage of financial issues within the reparable-management process. For further discussion of related defense financial policies, see Baldwin and Gotz, 1998; and Pint et al., 2002.

[23] The wholesale supply system acts as a "middle man" for logistics customers. It maintains inventories of spare parts to meet demands from customers by buying repairs from Army maintenance facilities or private-sector contractors and new parts from vendors.

[24] DLA and the other services set their own surcharge rates for the items they manage. Non-Army-managed items do not incur any additional surcharge from the Army.

least expensive option. Diversions of purchases may cause the AWCF to not fully recover all of its fixed costs, necessitating further surcharge increases. If the AWCF's actual sales volume is higher or lower than was expected when the surcharge rate was calculated, the AWCF will either overrecover or underrecover any fixed costs included in the surcharge.

An analysis of the supply-management surcharge shows that it includes fixed costs that do not vary with supply-management activity; these fixed costs could be funded by direct appropriations to avoid distorting customers' supply and repair decisions, while variable costs could be allocated more specifically to the items that generate them. Fixed costs include the costs of DoD agencies such as the Defense Logistics Services Center (DLSC), the Defense Automated Addressing System Center (DAASC), and the Defense Reutilization and Marketing Service (DRMS) (the agency referred to above in the discussion of disposal of condemned unserviceables); depreciation; and adjustments for prior-year losses or gains. Variable costs include depot storage and distribution costs, transportation costs, condemnation rates, and losses and obsolescence. In FY2000, a shift in funding such as that described here could have reduced the surcharge from 26.7 percent to 15.4 percent and provided direct funding of $136.5 million. This would imply a corresponding shift of $136.5 million from other accounts (e.g., Operations and Maintenance, Army (OMA)). In this case, the price charged the OMA customer for a $600,000 engine would be reduced by $53,000. All things being equal, the total cost to the Army would remain unchanged, but the marginal cost of each order would be more transparent.

Similarly, depot repair costs are based on computed depot-maintenance hourly labor rates, which include fixed costs that do not vary with repair activity and costs that could be allocated on an item-by-item basis. Fixed costs include Defense Information Systems Agency (DISA) and Defense Finance and Accounting Service (DFAS) bills, depreciation, rent, utilities, facilities maintenance, and prior-year gains or losses.[25] Fixed costs could be recovered through direct appropriations or lump-sum payments from customers. Variable costs that could be allocated on an item-by-item basis rather than on the basis of a labor-hour factor include spare parts, supplies, transportation and distribution, and equipment and engineering support provided for specific types of items. In FY2000, reprogramming these costs would have reduced the depot-maintenance hourly rate from $111.87 to $48.04. These changes would require revision of OSD policy.

The benefits associated with the direct funding of fixed costs include the following:

---

[25] Some proportion of these costs, such as utilities and facilities maintenance, could vary with maintenance activity and could be allocated on an item-by-item basis, using activity-based costing. The Army has used activity-based costing to develop installation-cost maps for intermediate-sustainment management (ISM) and for the service-based costing system for installation support services. See Brauner et al., 1997; and Tsai and Evanovich, 1999.

- Recovery of fixed costs is not dependent on demands being equal to forecasted value; fixed costs can be recovered with certainty, making it easier to keep the AWCF cash flows balanced.
- Increased visibility of fixed costs makes them subject to management scrutiny so that efforts to decrease costs will be clearly visible and those efforts can be rewarded.
- Customers can better identify what they are paying for—parts, labor, transportation, etc.
- No additional resources are required to implement direct funding.

Table 5.1 provides a generic example of cost allocation under the current pricing structure and shows how those same costs could be reallocated under marginal pricing (when fixed costs are directly funded). For this example, the DLR (an engine) originally cost the Army $400,000 (LAC). With current financial policies, a customer who requests a serviceable engine and returns a broken engine pays net $380,000. With marginal pricing, that same transaction would cost the customer $176,000, and the $204,000 for maintaining the fixed costs of the logistics infrastructure would be directly funded (and OMA or other accounts would be reduced by that amount).

Table 5.1
An Example of Current Cost Allocation vs. Marginal Cost Allocation (in dollars)

Item	Current Cost	Proposed Customer Cost	Proposed Direct Funded Cost
Engine			
LAC	400,000	400,000	
Surcharge (25%)	100,000		
Fixed costs			44,000
Supply management			
Depot management			
Headquarters management			
Infrastructure costs			
Variable costs (14%)		56,000	
Transportation			
Condemnation rate			
Obsolescence			
Army Master Data File (AMDF) price	500,000		160,000
Repair cost ($112/hr)			
Fixed costs ($64/hr)			
Facilities maintenance			
Utilities			
Variable costs ($48/hr)	120,000	120,000	
Direct labor			
Parts			
Engineering support			
Repair cost	280,000	120,000	
With unserviceable return, customer pays	380,000	176,000	

Exchange pricing, under which requests and returns are combined in the same financial transaction, offers another opportunity to improve the Army's financial policy for spare parts. Continuing with the same example, under current policy, the customer first obligates $500,000 (AMDF price) when the serviceable engine is requested. If the customer returns the broken engine to the supply system, his account will be credited with $120,000 (AMDF price minus surcharge minus repair cost). Under exchange pricing, the two transactions (request and return) would be combined into one financial transaction for $320,000. Under exchange pricing, there is no net difference in the total amount debited to the customer's account. The only difference is that there is one financial transaction, not two. Thus, exchange pricing reduces financial uncertainty and workload for both the customer and supply management.

In addition, in the current environment, Army maintenance depots have unused facilities and equipment capacity. Therefore, any additional use or marginal production of that capacity for repairing DLRs has the effect of spreading fixed costs over more transactions and thereby reducing the total cost per repair. As a result, apparently less-expensive DLR repairs below the depot level can have a financial consequence for the Army. Under the current pricing policies, a unit might decide that it would be cheaper to repair an item than to buy a serviceable one through standard supply channels. However, that economic decision must include the cost to the Army to operate the depot-level capability even if it is not used. The marginal cost-allocation approach is a direct attempt to bring that cost to the Army into the pricing presented to the customer.[26]

Conclusion

This chapter has identified several options for improving the Army's repair process. These options, along with those presented in Chapter Four, can help make the reparable-management process more responsive to customer needs. However, as with the process-improvement options discussed in the previous chapter, the repair-activities options are not of equal relevance or ease of implementation.

The frequent replanning and sharing of current information between the supply and repair activities is key to improved responsiveness. Within repair activities,

---

[26] The reliability of the repaired DLR should also be included in that economic decision analysis. For example, TACOM compared the mean operating hours between failures (MTBF) for M1A1 engines repaired by DS+ (a direct support repair capability at armor units), using a repair standard that calls for inspection and repair only as necessary (255 hrs), the depot using the DMWR for service-life-extension (SLE) engines (600 hrs), and depot repair to a newly developed national maintenance work requirement (NMWR) standard (800 hrs). Both the Army's fixed costs and the product's reliability are relevant to the customer's decision to repair locally or buy a replacement. However, the relevant information must be made available to enable the decisionmakers to make the right decisions.

mechanisms are needed to translate revised output schedules into internal shop signals regarding priorities.

The next most critical area for improvement is repair-part availability. The examples discussed related most directly to the case-study NIIN and shop environment. Not all the same issues will necessarily apply at the same levels for all NIINs. For example, the availability of unserviceable assets for induction varies by NIIN and may not be a critical factor to improvement in some cases.

There is near-universal acceptance that issues related to financial-management policy constrain the reparable-management process (as well as other logistics processes). However, those issues do not prevent efforts to improve the reparables process from moving forward. Financial-policy improvement can proceed in parallel with the logistics-process efforts.

CHAPTER SIX

Recommendations for Pilot Implementation

In this chapter, we summarize and structure the alternatives discussed above into a set of overarching recommendations for an initial pilot implementation. The reparable-management process for returning unserviceable assets to a serviceable condition to meet customer needs is complex and involves many stakeholders. Thus, our intent is to sketch an integrated approach that addresses some of the fundamental causes of the lack of adequate serviceable DLRs for issue to customers.

The Need for a More-Responsive Reparable-Management Process

For a process as complex as reparable management, the causes of the current unsatisfactory performance levels are certainly open to debate. While we have not attempted to identify either the root causes or the dominant causes of the problems, our case-study-based analysis identified evidence of some causal relationships, and we have proposed some alternative approaches to attain improvement.

The availability of reparables to customers can be dramatically improved without increased resources. Examples of ways to efficiently improve each area can be found in successful commercial practice, as well as in some isolated successes within military practice that deserve expansion.

The case study suggests a need to emphasize an integrated approach to planning and execution (i.e., frequent replanning), one that involves both the item-management team at the MSC and the depot-maintenance team. This analysis examines the management of availability of reparables to meet the dynamic needs of Army warfighters.[1] It assumes current DLR reliability, existing information technology at the MSC and the depot, available repair capabilities and capacity, and current DLR inventory-level (with the exception of safety-stock levels) determination meth-

---

[1] The reliability of reparable assets requires an inventory of serviceable spares to buffer the mission needs of the Army. The focus in this study has been on management of the availability of serviceable reparable assets and alternative approaches that could make the process more responsive to changing demand patterns.

odology and practices. In the long term, all of these assumptions are subject to challenge.

Recommendations for a Pilot Effort

Implementation of improvement initiatives can be made more tractable by starting with a pilot effort focused on DLRs for which there are applicable improvement alternatives. Because this analysis focuses on the reparables process, the activities involved include a vertical slice of interdependent activities at both the MSC and the supporting depot. Therefore, alternatives potentially cross organizational and functional boundaries. With a pilot implementation effort, limited permission can be granted to try new procedures and policy proposals in a "laboratory" setting, thereby reducing the risk of change for the larger organization. Results can be measured, rules adjusted, and confidence developed before widespread change is implemented. Of course, practical mechanisms must be developed to apply the successful and proven concepts to a broader workload. With literally thousands of reparable NIINs potentially involved, full implementation of the desired changes will take careful planning and time.

The overall measure of success would be a reduction in the number and duration of BOs for the selected NIINs without exceeding the serviceable inventory levels needed to meet customer requirements. Therefore, both BO rates and CWT should be used as performance metrics.

We recommend that senior management at an MSC appoint a small pilot implementation team that focuses initially on a few reparable NIINs related to a single weapon system or end-item that is repaired at the same facility.

Following the discussion in Chapters Four and Five, we recommend that the pilot implementation should

- Address uncertainty concerns.
- Properly link long-term planning and replanning for responsive execution.
- Improve repair responsiveness.

The first two recommendations focus extensively on the managing MSC. The third primarily concerns the supporting repair activities. However, the MSC and the repair depot need to work as a team to improve the overall process by integrating and synchronizing their efforts.

The discussion that follows expands briefly on each of the alternatives described earlier. Interactions exist among the alternatives, and care is required to ensure that the initiatives implemented are sufficiently complementary to achieve the desired level of improvement. The level of such interaction may vary, depending on the

NIINs chosen for the pilot program. For example, in the case study, merely improving the responsiveness of replanning and changes to repair PRON quantities was not sufficient when the parts available to support the repair also had deficiencies. While coordination or synchronization of implementation may not necessarily be required for individual alternatives, it may often be necessary to ease more than one constraint simultaneously; alternatively, the easing of a constraint can permit the clear visibility of the next constraint.

Addressing Uncertainty

We recommend addressing uncertainty in four ways:

1. Use current forecast models while looking to future improvement.
2. Use revised monthly forecasts for near-term decisions.
3. Selectively adjust DLR safety stock.
4. Implement strategies that shorten lead times.

First, we suggest continued use of the current forecasting model in the RD&ES module. In the long term, the Army should evaluate all such decision models with the aim of developing and implementing improvements, but there is no evidence that a dramatically improved forecasting tool is available at this time. The limitations of the current model are associated with the long planning horizons required for the budget and other long-term planning tasks. Therefore, the best basic approach is frequent replanning using revised forecasts based on current data, where possible. The already-implemented move to monthly execution of RD&ES against the reparable items is thus the appropriate approach.

Second, in the near term, it will be important to place greater emphasis on use of the monthly production projections from the current RD&ES module of CCSS. The activities at both the MSC and the depot require revised (near-term-horizon) forecasts of production needs. In addition, adjustments can also help prevent overproduction when demand declines. For example, not only does the depot repair shop need to know the revised number of units required for the month, it must also be recognized that the IM will often need that output delivered to DLA distribution centers more frequently than just once at the end of the month. Provisions are needed to facilitate direct discussion between the IM and the depot scheduling clerk or shop chief to negotiate desires and limitations that will benefit the customer. Existing e-mail and telephone capability could be used.

Third, selective adjustment of safety-stock levels for some DLRs could have an immediate impact on responsiveness (i.e., CWT). It is not initially necessary to change safety-level policy for Army DLRs. The implementation team need only analyze and determine a level for pilot implementation that recognizes the realities associated with a specific NIIN and then evaluate the impact the stock level has on customer requirements and the ability of stock to better accommodate demand uncertainty.

Finally, the same analysis that informs the decision on safety stock should produce an initial target for effectively shortening the repair lead time for a given NIIN. There is interaction between operating stock, safety stock, and repair lead times, and thus a coordinated strategy is called for. Moreover, revisions to both parameters should be possible over time as various activities and conditions improve throughout the process. For example, lower repair lead times reduce the need for operating stock; faster repair can substitute for inventory investment.

As progress is made to improve customer support, it will also be important to update the data in the CCSS database for the NIIN, so that better revised monthly forecasts are available to permit informed decisions. While the examples presented here have emphasized reducing customer BOs, it is just as important in the long run to prevent unnecessary repairs that place a NIIN in a long supply condition (i.e., the accumulation of serviceable assets above the desired inventory level). As an example, when programmed changes to fielding densities are not updated in the database, the model calculus will not properly reflect desired inventory levels.

The approaches recommended here address issues similar to those that should be considered and communicated during a thorough monthly supply-control study. However, our recommendations raise some specific issues and parameters that were not being considered when we analyzed the M88A1 engine case study: safety stock, lead-time strategies, and direct contact with the source of repair. While this may sound complex and time-consuming when considered for each DLR, the real complexity rests in the initial analysis for the NIIN. Once the strategy for that NIIN is determined, monthly effort can focus on communication with the depot and database-maintenance actions. Mechanisms such as e-mail could be the basis for improved communication between IMs and repair supervisors. The key issue here is to make repair-program execution activities that respond directly to customer demands the first priority for those involved. These strategies do not reduce variability in demand over the planning horizon. Rather, they mitigate the impact of that variability.

Properly Linking Long-Term Planning and Replanning for Responsive Execution

We recommend properly linking the management of long-term planning and near-term execution:

1. Long-term planning
    a. Focus on budget and capacity-planning activities.
    b. Revise the future program basis at least quarterly.
2. Near-term replanning
    a. Focus on responsive execution and metrics that reflect customer support at least monthly.

   b. Take a NIIN-level and customer-needs view.
   c. Link production output to actual customer demands.
   d. Decentralize execution decisionmaking.

Long-term planning activities must continue to address the needs of budget development and capacity planning. These activities deliberately call for long planning horizons. We are advocating the use of revised forecasts to revise planned PRONs and other actions as new information becomes available. The long-term planning tasks exist to take imperfect predictions of future requirements and plan the best response possible that can meet those requirements. Therefore, near-term *replanning* actions are critical.

The emphasis recommended here brings the focus of the IM and the repair depot to the daily task of responding to the warfighter's requirements. CWT should be a key metric. How long the customer waits for the need to be satisfied and the consistency of that service level are important. Metrics such as BO rates provide further, deeper insight into causation. However, visibility of customer needs is key to responding effectively. Between the SSF implementation and the improved visibility of tactical customers through the Integrated Logistics Analysis Program (ILAP) and the ADM website, the IM has a better view of the requirement and now needs a path to improvement. The near-term alternatives link repair production to sales and needs by using the monthly RD&ES output to pull just enough production for the NIIN to meet and sustain the current demand. As lead time is reduced, the IM will need mechanisms to share sales information even more frequently with the repair shop so that it can respond effectively. The implementation team will need to revise policies and procedures that will enable IM and repair personnel to operate promptly at acceptable risk to achieve the desired results. There is clearly an implication that some decisions will be decentralized or will be permitted outside the current decision chain.

Procedures and bounds will need to be developed, and some training may be required. However, a systematized decision structure is envisioned that is still much more flexible than the current structure. The key is in the small incremental adjustments that would be involved with the shorter decision horizons associated with replanning. Most IMs already make incremental decisions daily to allocate scarce DLR resources among customers awaiting assets. The decisions envisioned would be no more complex or risky, but the goal would be to focus the IM's efforts on maintaining defined levels of stock so that the CCSS software logic can handle the DLR allocations from the available serviceable inventory. There are still decision constraints around PRONs, shop capacity, etc. Within the bounds of those constraints, incremental decisions that improve customer support are the objective.

However, effective planning alone does not put serviceable assets on the shelf. The case study showed that improvements are also needed in the repair environment.

Improving Repair Responsiveness

The designated repair activity must have the capability and capacity to respond promptly if the overall process is to effectively and efficiently meet customer needs. We recommend addressing improvements to repair responsiveness in four ways:

1. Production and scheduling controls
    a. Use pull production scheduling.
    b. Improve controls on WIP.
    c. Reduce lead time to complete repair of the next asset and continuously reduce overall repair flow time.
2. Repair parts availability
    a. Revise current DOS policy to add diversity, depending on different NIIN characteristics.
    b. Make demand-based investment decisions.
3. Unserviceables availability
    a. Improve asset turn-in and retrograde.
4. Financial policies
    a. Ensure that any carryover workload addresses current customer demands, not customer BOs.
    b. Improve economic transparency.
    c. Evaluate and pilot net and marginal pricing.

The first requirement for success is the ability to accept changes in workload, integrate them into the affected work centers, and ensure that all workload requirements can continue to be met over time. The long-term planning and PRON approval include coordination with the maintenance depot. In addition, the more frequent replanning and coordination described above provide a continuing dialogue on the incremental changes to the schedules. Therefore, as long as the depot planning activity and the work-center schedulers and supervisors are kept informed on a continuing basis, the depot will be aware of the critical constraints and can be proactive about developing alternatives to ease the critical constraints in time to accommodate customer needs.

The alternative we recommend calls for the work-center scheduling clerk and the repair supervisor to use the revised production requirements from the IM to adjust the production schedule and repair-parts ordering. The most significant change would be the shift to a pull schedule, which can reduce lead time, provide flexibility for dealing with demand changes, and protect against overproduction when demand slows. A pull schedule is also relatively easy to manage with minimal IT requirements.

Lead-time reduction to improve the responsiveness of the repair activities should deal with time until the completion of the next repair and also reduction of the overall repair flow time. The pull scheduling and production-control techniques would facilitate these efforts.

The second issue that must be addressed is that of assuring the availability of sufficient repair parts for every task required in the repair procedure. The pull scheduling approach provides one option for addressing this issue. Stock should be issued to repair technicians at their work locations, and "kitting" of parts for NIIN repair at a location should be pursued to the maximum extent possible. In addition, all parts used in support of DLR repair should be ordered as recurring-demand materiel so that the demand history is provided to the relevant IMs for planning vendor replenishment. The ASRS provides critical control and visibility for both new repair parts and serviceable reclaimed material. Provision should exist for the use of a local-purchase credit card for prompt resolution of part shortages for material backordered from the national provider. Such purchases should be only for quantities sufficient to meet schedules and customer needs (i.e., responsive repair quantities).

After the depot has brought its inventories under better control, better coordination and support for new repair parts from the IMs will be needed in AMC and DLA. The coding of parts as recurring demands is the first important step toward providing more-accurate information to IMs. That information clarifies the need for continuing vendor support. However, the IM for the DLR NIIN also has parts-consumption data about low-usage items that are still necessary for support of the DLR. These data need to be coordinated with the appropriate IMs so they can determine inventory and vendor availability. In some cases, the Army may decide to buy assets for depot shop-stock inventory as insurance for future availability. The IMs must also be aware of vendor lead times for items to ensure that either vendor relationships are in place or that procurement actions are taken in time to support the repair programs.

The costs associated with low-usage and long-lead-time parts are some of the highest investment costs to support DLRs (after the cost of the DLR itself). A 60-DOS policy may not be nearly sufficient with respect to such items. On the other hand, many items used on nearly every repair and ordered frequently as recurring demand could be stocked at less than 60 DOS. Furthermore, the scheduling initiative described above will both reduce WIP and provide shorter repair-cycle times that together may permit reductions in future DLR investments.

As the overall reparable process becomes more responsive to the customer, the issue of the availability of unserviceables will become more apparent. The limited availability of some DLRs has already increased the need for improved flow through the reverse logistics pipeline for the retrograde of these unserviceable assets. However, for some DLRs for older current systems, "excess" unserviceable carcasses are the most efficient source of critical repair parts. Furthermore, the importance of an efficient reverse pipeline will grow as the Army's maintenance transformation to two-level maintenance progresses.

Finally, the financial policies related to reparables need to be aligned with sending signals to customers and all the other participants in the process. Individuals throughout the Army try to do the right thing. In the absence of full and correct information, they try to act rationally in their local context. The challenge is to recognize and acknowledge just how motivated some individuals are and to give them the information they need to make logical decisions in the best interest of the Army at large, not just the local situation. The current practice for handling carryover workload is an example of an incentive within the maintenance depot that tends to stretch out repair completions.

Conclusion

The recommendations discussed here comprise a coherent set of interdependent initiatives that should be pursued as a pilot implementation that vertically integrates the IM and the depot-level repair work centers. Specifics will necessarily differ among DLRs. However, we recommend the immediate undertaking of a pilot implementation to verify concepts, prototype procedures, and develop confidence in expanding the implementation rapidly within a depot, across depots, and across MSCs.

In the future, demands could eventually decrease because the quality of DLR repair will improve with common repair standards occurring at fewer locations. If demands decline and repair locations are further consolidated, systemwide cost savings should result. Excess maintenance capacity and the associated resources can both be reduced.

As with all process-change efforts, the devil is in the details. That is precisely the strength of a recommendation for a pilot implementation effort. Experimentation, performance measurement, and analytical feedback for continuous adjustment and improvement are envisioned. Whether the improvement methodology used is the DMI methodology illustrated in Figure 1.1 or the methodologies incorporated in the lean-manufacturing or six-sigma approaches, these iterative continuous-improvement techniques will identify the detailed issues that must be resolved. Improvement actions can be initiated before a complete, optimal plan of action is developed.

As the reparable-management process improves, some trends should begin to emerge. The underlying intent of this effort is to provide significantly more-responsive service to the ultimate customer. The application of lean-thinking concepts to processes normally provides dramatic improvements in both throughput effectiveness and efficiency. The expectation is that excess repair capacity will be eliminated while responsiveness to customer demands improves. The greater use of depot capacity should help with fixed-cost absorption at those locations. A single standard of DLR repair under the NMWR approach could assure improved performance and improved overall MTBF even before basic reengineering of component reliability is addressed. Together, the efficiency improvements should result in cost reductions throughout the Army.

Bibliography[1]

Abell, J. B., G. M. Carter, K. E. Isaacson, and T. F. Lippiatt, *Estimating Requirements for Aircraft Recoverable Spares and Depot Repair*, Santa Monica, CA: RAND Corporation, R-4210-AF, 1993.

Air Force Materiel Command Instruction 21-129, "Depot Maintenance Management, Depot Repair Enhancement Process (DREP)," Headquarters, Air Force Materiel Command, Department of the Air Force, Wright-Patterson Air Force Base, Ohio, March 9, 2001.

American Management Association, *Blueprints for Service Quality: The Federal Express Approach*, 3d ed., New York: AMA Publications, 1997.

American Production and Inventory Control Society, Remanufacturing Seminar, Salt Lake City, Utah, September 1992.

Army Regulation 750-1, "Army Materiel Maintenance Policy and Retail Maintenance Operations," Headquarters, Department of the Army, Washington, DC, July 1, 1996.

Baldwin, Laura, and Glenn Gotz, *Transfer Pricing for Air Force Depot-Level Reparables*, Santa Monica, CA: RAND Corporation, MR-808-AF, 1998.

Blackburn, J. D., *Time-Based Competition: The Next Battle in American Manufacturing*, Homewood, IL: Irwin Business One, 1991.

Brauner, Marygail K., J. Bondanella, et al., *ISM-X: Evaluation and Policy Implications*, Santa Monica, CA: RAND Corporation, MR-829-A, 1997.

Brauner, Marygail K., Ellen M. Pint, John R. Bondanella, Daniel A. Relles, Paul Steinberg, and Rick Eden, *Evaluating Five Proposed Price and Credit Policies for the Army*, Santa Monica, CA: RAND Corporation, DB-291-A, 2000.

Brauner, Marygail K., Ellen M. Pint, Daniel A. Relles, and Paul Steinberg, *Dollars and Sense: A Process Improvement Approach to Logistics Financial Management*, Santa Monica, CA: RAND Corporation, MR-1131-A, 2000.

---

[1] Most RAND documents are available at http://www.rand.org.

Byrne, P. M., and W. J. Markham, *Improving Quality and Productivity in the Logistics Process: Achieving Customer Satisfaction Breakthroughs*, Oak Brook, IL: Council of Logistics Management, 1991.

Cohen, I. K., John B. Abell, and T. Lippiatt, *Coupling Logistics to Operations to Meet Uncertainty and the Threat (CLOUT): An Overview*, Santa Monica, CA: RAND Corporation, R-3979-AF, 1991.

Cohen, I. K., David Kassing, J. Bondanella, and James R. Chiesa, *Issues in Materiel Distribution: A Background Note*, Santa Monica, CA: RAND Corporation, N-2791-P&L, 1989.

Crawford, G. B., *Variability in the Demands for Aircraft Spare Parts: Its Magnitude and Implications*, Santa Monica, CA: RAND Corporation, R-3318-AF, 1988.

CWT and RWT Metrics Measure the Performance of the Army's Logistics Chain for Spare Parts, Santa Monica, CA: RAND Corporation, RB-3035-A, 2003.

Define, Measure, Improve: The Change Methodology That Has Propelled the Army's Successful Velocity Management Initiative, Santa Monica, CA: RAND Corporation, RB-3020, 2000.

Delurgio, S., *Forecasting Principles and Applications*, Burr Ridge, IL: Irwin/McGraw-Hill, 1998.

Department of Defense, Financial Management Regulation, DoD 7000.14-R, Washington, DC.

Department of Defense, *Secondary Item Stratification Manual*, DoD 4110.1-M, Washington, DC, June 1995.

"Depot Maintenance Reengineering," *Air Force Journal of Logistics, Special Features*, Vol. 27, No. 1, Spring 2003.

Diener, David, Eric Peltz, Arthur Lackey, Darlene J. Blake, and Karthik Vaidyanathan, *Value Recovery from the Reverse Logistics Pipeline*, Santa Monica, CA: RAND Corporation, MG-238-A, 2004.

Dougherty, John, *Inventory Reduction Report*, New York, NY: Institute of Management and Administration, July 2001.

Drucker, P., "Drucker on Management: A Turnaround Primer," *Wall Street Journal*, February 1, 1993, p. A14.

Dumond, John, Marygail K. Brauner, Rick Eden, et al., *Velocity Management: The Business Paradigm That Has Transformed U.S. Army Logistics*, Santa Monica, CA: RAND Corporation, MR-1108-A, 2001.

Dumond, John, Rick Eden, and John R. Folkeson, *Velocity Management: An Approach for Improving the Responsiveness and Efficiency of Army Logistics Processes*, Santa Monica, CA: RAND Corporation, DB-126-1-1, 1995.

Eden, Rick, et al., "Reinventing the DoD Logistics System to Support Military Operations in the Post-Cold War Era," in Paul K. Davis (ed.), *New Challenges for Defense Planning: Rethinking How Much Is Enough*, Santa Monica, CA: RAND Corporation, 1994, pp. 699–725.

Edwards, T. J., and R. Eden, "Velocity Management and the Revolution in Military Logistics," *Army Logistician,* Vol. 31, Issue 1, January–February 1999, pp. 52–57.

Frangos, S. J., and S. J. Bennett, *Team Zebra,* Essex Junction, VT: Oliver Wright Publications, Inc., 1993.

GAO, *Air Force Depot Maintenance: Budget Difficulties and Operational Inefficiencies,* NSIAD-00-185, Washington, DC, August 15, 2000.

GAO, *Army Inventory: Growth in Inventories That Exceed Requirements,* NSIAD-90-68, Washington, DC, March 1990a.

GAO, *Army Inventory: Parts Shortages Are Impacting Operations and Maintenance Effectiveness,* NSIAD-01-772, Washington, DC, July 2001a.

GAO, *Army Maintenance: Clearer Guidance Needed to Ensure Programs Reflect Current Requirements,* NSIAD-90-229, Washington, DC, August 13, 1990b.

GAO, *Commercial Practices: DoD Could Save Millions by Reducing Maintenance and Repair Inventories,* NSIAD-93-155, Washington, DC, June 1993.

GAO, *Defense Working Capital Fund: Improvements Needed for Managing the Backlog of Funded Work,* GAO-01-559, Washington, DC, May 30, 2001b.

GAO, *Department of Defense: Status of Financial Management Weaknesses and Progress Toward Reform,* GAO-03-931T, Washington, DC, June 25, 2003.

GAO, *Status of Efforts to Implement Personnel Reductions in the Army Materiel Command,* Washington, DC, March 1999.

Georgoff, D. M., and R. G. Murdick, "Managers Guide to Forecasting," *Harvard Business Review,* January–February 1986.

Gitlow, H. S., and S. J. Gitlow, *The Deming Guide to Quality and Competitive Position,* Englewood Cliffs, NJ: Prentice-Hall, 1987.

The Global Logistics Research Team, Michigan State University, *World Class Logistics: The Challenge of Managing Continuous Change,* Oak Brook, IL: Council of Logistics Management, 1995.

Goldratt, E. M., *It's Not Luck,* Great Barrington, MA: North River Press, 1994.

Goldratt, E. M., *Theory of Constraints,* New York: North River Press, 1990.

Goldratt, E. M., and J. Cox, *The Goal,* Croton-on-the-Hudson, NY: North River Press, 1984.

Hammer, M., and J. Champy, *Reengineering the Corporation,* New York: Harper Collins, 1993.

Hillier, F. S., and G. J. Lieberman, *Introduction to Operations Research,* 7th ed., New York: McGraw-Hill, 2001.

Hix, William M., J. Bondanella, Bruce J. Held, et al., *Options for Managing the Army's Arsenals and Ammunition Plants,* Santa Monica, CA: RAND Corporation, DB-353-A, 2003.

Hix, William M., Ellen M. Pint, J. Bondanella, et al., *Rethinking Governance of the Army's Arsenals and Ammunition Plants*, Santa Monica, CA: RAND Corporation, MR-1651-A, 2003.

Hodges, James S., and Raymond A. Pyles, *Onward Through the Fog: Uncertainty and Management Adaptation in Systems Analysis and Design*, Santa Monica, CA: RAND Corporation, R-3760, 1990.

Imai, M., *Kaizen: The Key to Japan's Competitive Success*, New York: McGraw Hill, 1986.

Johnson, H. T., and R. S. Kaplan, *Relevance Lost: The Rise and Fall of Management Accounting*, Boston, MA: Harvard Business School Press, 1987.

Jones, D. T., *Lean Thinking: Banish Waste and Create Wealth in Your Corporation*, New York: Simon and Schuster, 1996.

Juran, J. M., *Juran on Planning for Quality*, New York: The Free Press, 1988.

Kaplan, R. S., and D. P. Norton, *The Balanced Scorecard: Translating Strategy into Action*, Boston, MA: Harvard Business School Press, 1996.

Kearns, D. T., and D. A. Nadler, *Prophets in the Dark*, New York: Harper Collins, 1992.

Keen, P.G.W., *The Process Edge: Creating Value Where It Counts*, Boston, MA: Harvard Business School Press, 1997.

Lepore, D., and O. Cohen, *Deming and Goldratt: The Theory of Constraints and the System of Profound Knowledge*, Great Barrington, MA: North River Press, 1999.

Levine, A., and J. Luck, *The New Management Paradigm*, Santa Monica, CA: RAND, MR-458-AF, 1994.

Makridakis, S., and S. C. Wheelwright, *Interactive Forecasting: Univariate and Multivariate Methods*, 2nd ed., San Francisco, CA: Holden-Day, 1978.

Mentzer, John T., and Carol C. Bienstock, *Sales Forecasting Management: Understanding the Techniques, Systems and Management of the Sales Forecasting Process*, Thousand Oaks, CA: Sage Publications, 1998.

Office of Management and Budget, Circular A-34, Department of Defense Directive 7200.1, Washington, DC.

Osborne, D., and T. Gaebler, *Reinventing Government: How the Entrepreneurial Spirit Is Transforming the Public Sector*, Reading, MA: Addison-Wesley Publishing Co., Inc., 1992.

Pagonis, W. G., with J. L. Cruikshank, *Moving Mountains: Lessons in Leadership and Logistics from the Gulf War*, Cambridge, MA: Harvard University Press, 1992.

Peltz, Eric, Marc L. Robbins, Patricia Boren, and Melvin Wolff, *Diagnosing the Army's Equipment Readiness: The Equipment Downtime Analyzer*, Santa Monica, CA: RAND Corporation, MR-1481-A, 2002.

Pint, Ellen M., Marygail K. Brauner, J. Bondanella, Daniel A. Relles, and Paul Steinberg, *Right Price, Fair Credit: Criteria to Improve Financial Incentives for Army Logistics Decisions*, Santa Monica, CA: RAND Corporation, MR-1150-A, 2002.

Pyzdek, T., *The Complete Guide to Six Sigma*, Tucson, AZ: QA Publishing, 1999.

Ried, P. C., *Well Made in America: Lessons from Harley-Davidson on Being the Best*, New York: McGraw-Hill, 1989.

Senge, Peter, *The Fifth Discipline: The Art and Practice of the Learning Organization*, New York: Currency Doubleday, 1990.

Sephehri, M., *Just-in-Time, Not Just in Japan, Case Studies of American Pioneers in JIT Implementation*, Falls Church, VA: American Production and Inventory Control Society, Inc., 1986.

Sherbrooke, C. C., *Optimal Inventory Modeling Systems: Multi-Echelon Techniques*, New York: Wiley, 1992.

Speeding the Flow: How the Army Cut Order-and-Ship Time, Santa Monica, CA: RAND Corporation, RB-3006, 1998.

Stalk, G., Jr., and T. M. Hout, *Competing Against Time: How Time Based Competition Is Reshaping Global Markets*, The Free Press, 1990.

Stevenson, W. J., *Operations Management*, 7th ed., New York: McGraw-Hill Companies, Inc., 2002.

Thor, C. G., "The Evolution of Performance Measurement in Government," *Journal of Cost Management*, May/June 2000, pp. 18–26.

Tsai, Michael J., and Peter Evanovich, *Evaluating the Use of Contractors for Installation Support Using Service Based Cost Data*, Alexandria, VA: Institute for Defense Analyses, 1999.

Wang, M.Y.D., *Accelerated Logistics: Streamlining the Army's Supply Chain*, Santa Monica, CA: RAND Corporation, MR-1140-A, 2000.

Womack, J. P., et al., *The Machine That Changed the World*, New York: Harper Perennial, 1991.

Womack, J. P., and D. T. Jones, *Lean Thinking: Banish Waste and Create Wealth in Your Corporation*, New York: Simon and Schuster, 1996.